How to Use Qualitative Methods in Evaluation

D0054720

Michael Quinn Patton

Center for the Study of Evaluation
University of California, Los Angeles

SAGE PUBLICATIONS
International Educational and Professional Publisher
Newbury Park London New Delhi

The second edition of the *Program Evaluation Kit* was developed at the Center for the Study of Evaluation, Graduate School of Education, University of California, Los Angeles.

The development of this second edition of the CSE *Program Evaluation Kit* was supported in part by a grant from the National Institute of Education, currently known as the Office of Educational Research and Improvement. However, the opinions expressed herein do not necessarily reflect the position or policy of that agency and no official endorsement should be inferred.

The second edition of the *Program Evaluation Kit* is published and distributed by Sage Publications, Inc., Newbury Park, California, under an exclusive agreement with The Regents of the University of California.

For information address:

 SAGE Publications, Inc.
2455 Teller Road
Newbury Park, California 91320
E-mail: order@sagepub.com

SAGE Publications Ltd.
6 Bonhill Street
London EC2A 4PU
United Kingdom

SAGE Publications India Pvt. Ltd.
M-32 Market
Greater Kailash I
New Delhi 110 048 India

Printed in the United States of America

Library of Congress Cataloging-in-Publication Data

Patton, Michael Quinn
    How to use qualitative methods in evaluation / Michael Quinn Patton.
       p.   cm.—(Program evaluation kit (2nd ed.); v. 4)
    Bibliography: p.
    Includes index.
    ISBN 0-8039-3129-8 (pbk.)
    1. Social sciences—Methodology. 2. Evaluation research (Social action programs). I. Title. II. Series.
H62.P3216   1987
361.6'1'072—dc19   87-21772
                  CIP

98 99 20 19

Contents

Acknowledgments

The preparation of this second edition of the Center for the Study of Evaluation *Program Evaluation Kit* has been a challenging task, made possible only through the combined efforts of a number of individuals.

First and foremost, Drs. Lynn Lyons Morris and Carol Taylor Fitz-Gibbon, the authors and editor of the original Kit. Together, they authored all eight of the original volumes, an enormous undertaking that required incredible knowledge, dedication, persistence, and painstaking effort. Lynn also worked relentlessly as editor of the entire set. Having struggled through only a revision, I stand in great awe of Lynn's and Carol's enormous accomplishment. This second edition retains much of their work and obviously would not have been possible without them.

Thanks also are due to Gene V Glass, Ernie House, Michael Q. Patton, Carol Weiss, and Robert Boruch, who reviewed our plans and offered specific assistance in targeting needed revisions. The work would not have proceeded without Marvin C. Alkin, who planted the seeds for the second edition and collaborated very closely during the initial planning phases.

I would like to acknowledge especially the contribution and help of Michael Q. Patton. True to form, Michael was an excellent, utilization-focused formative evaluator for the final draft manuscript, carefully responding to our work and offering innumerable specific suggestions for its improvement. We have incorporated into the *Handbook* his framework for differentiating among kinds of evaluation studies (formative, summative, implementation, outcomes).

Many staff members at the Center for the Study of Evaluation contributed to the production of the Kit. The entire effort was supervised by Aeri Lee, able office manager at the Center. Katherine Fry, word processing expert, was able to accomplish incredible graphic feats for the *Handbook* and tirelessly labored on manuscript production and data transfer. Ruth Paysen, who was a major contributor to the production of the original Kit, also was a painstaking and dedicated proofreader for the second edition. Margie Franco, Tori Gouveia, and Katherine Lu also participated in the production effort.

Marie Freeman and Pamela Aschbacher, also from the Center, contributed their ideas, editorial skills, and endless examples. Carli

Rogers, of UCLA Contracts and Grants, was both caring and careful in her negotiations for us.

At Sage Publications, thanks to Sara McCune for her encouragement and to Mitch Allen for his nudging and patience.

And at the Center for the Study of Evaluation, the project surely would not have been possible without Eva L. Baker, Director. Eva is a continuing source of encouragement, ideas, support, fun, and friendship.

—Joan L. Herman
Center for the Study of Evaluation
University of California, Los Angeles

Chapter 1
An Introduction to Qualitative Methods

Qualitative methods consist of three kinds of data collection: (1) in-depth, open-ended interviews; (2) direct observation; and (3) written documents, including such sources as open-ended written items on questionnaires, personal diaries, and program records. The data from open-ended interviews consist of direct quotations from people about their experiences, opinions, feelings, and knowledge. The data from observations consist of detailed descriptions of program activities, participants' behaviors, staff actions, and the full range of human interactions that can be part of program experiences. Document analysis yields excerpts, quotations, or entire passages from records, correspondence, official reports, and open-ended surveys.

Qualitative evaluation data begin as raw, descriptive information about programs and people in programs. The evaluator visits the program to make firsthand observations of program activities, sometimes even engaging personally in those activities as a "participant observer." The evaluator talks with participants and staff about their experiences and perceptions. Records and documents are usually also examined. The data from these interviews, observations, and documents are then organized into major themes, categories, and case examples through content analysis.

A typical qualitative evaluation report will provide the following:

- detailed description of program implementation;
- analysis of major program processes;
- description of different types of participants and different kinds of participation;
- descriptions of how the program has affected participants;
- observed changes (or lack thereof), outcomes, and impacts; and

- analysis of program strengths and weaknesses as reported by people interviewed (e.g., participants, staff, funders, key informants in the community).

Qualitative evaluation data may be presented alone or in combination with quantitative data. Recent developments in the evaluation profession have led to an increase in the use of multiple methods including combinations of qualitative and quantitative data.

The validity and reliability of qualitative data depend to a great extent on the methodological skill, sensitivity, and training of the evaluator. Systematic and rigorous observation involves far more than just being present and looking around. Skillful interviewing involves much more than just asking questions. Content analysis requires considerably more than just reading to see what's there. Generating useful and credible qualitative evaluation data through observation, interviewing, and content analysis requires discipline, knowledge, training, practice, and hard work.

This chapter provides an introduction to qualitative evaluation approaches. Later chapters describe when to use qualitative methods in evaluation; how to design a qualitative evaluation; how to use observational methods; how to conduct in-depth, open-ended interviews; and how to analyze qualitative data. The final chapter discusses philosophical and political issues related to qualitative methods, including a review of the debate about the credibility and scientific value of qualitative evaluations.

The next section places the decision to use qualitative methods within the larger context of making methods decisions in evaluation.

Making Methods Decisions

Before considering the strengths and weaknesses of qualitative methods, it is useful to place the decision to gather qualitative data within the larger context of evaluation decisions generally. The nine volumes of the *Program Evaluation Kit* focus on different parts of the evaluation process and varying approaches to evaluation.

Data collection options and strategies for any particular evaluation depend on answers to several questions:

(1) *Who* is the information for and *who* will use the findings of the evaluation?
(2) *What* kinds of information are needed?

(3) *How* is the information to be used? For what purposes is evaluation being done?
(4) *When* is the information needed?
(5) *What* resources are available to conduct the evaluation?

Answers to these questions will determine the kinds of data that are appropriate in a particular evaluation. The challenge in evaluation is getting the best possible information to the people who need it—and then *getting those people to actually use the information in decision making.*

There are no rigid rules that can be provided for making data collection and methods decisions in evaluation. The art of evaluation involves creating a design and gathering information that is appropriate for a specific situation and particular policymaking context. In art there is no single, ideal standard. Beauty is in the eye of the beholder, and the evaluation beholders include a variety of stakeholders: decision makers, policymakers, funders, program managers, staff, program participants, and the general public. Any given design is necessarily an interplay of resources, practicalities, methodological choices, creativity, and personal judgments by the people involved.

Qualitative and Quantitative Data Choices

Considering evaluation design alternatives leads directly to consideration of the relative strengths and weaknesses of qualitative and quantitative data. Qualitative methods permit the evaluator to study selected issues, cases, or events in depth and detail; the fact that data collection is not constrained by predetermined categories of analysis contributes to the depth and detail of qualitative data. Quantitative methods, on the other hand, use standardized measures that fit diverse various opinions and experiences into predetermined response categories. The advantage of the quantitative approach is that it measures the reactions of a great many people to a limited set of questions, thus facilitating comparison and statistical aggregation of the data. This gives a broad, generalizable set of findings. By contrast, qualitative methods typically produce a wealth of detailed data about a much smaller number of people and cases. Qualitative data provide depth and detail through direct quotation and careful description of program situations, events, people, interactions, and observed behaviors. The detailed descriptions, direct quotations, and case documentation of qualitative methods are collected as open-ended narrative without attempting to fit program activities or peoples' experiences into predetermined, standardized categories such as the response choices that constitute typical questionnaires or tests.

An Illustrative Comparison at the Simplest Level

In collecting qualitative data, the evaluator seeks to capture the richness of people's experiences in their own terms. Understanding and meaning emerge from in-depth analysis of detailed descriptions and verbatim quotations. To illustrate at the simplest level what is meant by depth, detail, and meaning in qualitative methods, compare one teacher's responses to a closed and open question on a mail survey. The first response is taken from a standardized item on the questionnaire.

Accountability as practiced in our school system creates an undesirable atmosphere of anxiety among teachers.

        _____ 1. strongly agree
        _____ 2. agree
        _____ 3. disagree
        _____ 4. strongly disagree

This teacher marked "strongly agree." Now compare the teacher's response on the above survey item to her response to an open-ended question.

Question: Please add any personal comments you'd like to make in your own words about any part of the school system's accountability approach.
Teacher's Response: "Fear" is the word for "accountability" as applied in our system.

My teaching before "Accountability" was the same as now. "Accountability" is a political ploy to maintain power. Whatever good there may have been in it in the beginning has been destroyed by the awareness that each new educational "system" has at its base a political motive. Students get screwed . . .

The bitterness and hatred in our system is incredible. What began as "noble" has been destroyed. You wouldn't believe the new layers of administration that have been created just to keep this monster going.

Our finest compliment around our state is that other school systems know what is going on and are having none of it. Lucky people.

Come down and visit in hell sometime.

These two questionnaire responses illustrate one kind of difference that can exist between qualitative data derived from responses to open-ended questions and quantitative measurement based on scales composed of standardized questionnaire items. Quantitative measures are succinct, parsimonious, and easily aggregated for analysis; they are systematic, standardized, and easily presented in a short space. By contrast, qualitative responses are longer, more detailed, and variable in content; analysis is difficult because responses are neither systematic nor standardized. Yet the open-ended response permits one to understand the world as seen by the respondent. The purpose of gathering responses to open-ended questions is to permit the evaluator to understand and capture the perspective of program participants without predetermining their perspective through prior selection of questionnaire categories.

Direct quotations are a basic source of raw data in qualitative evaluation. Direct quotations reveal the respondents' levels of emotion, the way in which they have organized the world, their thoughts about what is happening, their experiences, and their basic perceptions. The task for the qualitative evaluator is to provide a framework within which people can respond in a way that represents accurately and thoroughly their point of view about the program.

It is important to note that open-ended responses on questionnaires represent the most elementary form of qualitative data. There are severe limitations to open-ended data collected in writing on questionnaires, limitations related to the writing skills of the persons completing the questionnaire. Yet even at this simple, elementary level of measurement, the feelings revealed in the open-ended comments of a single teacher illustrate the power and depth of qualitative data.

It is important to keep in mind that the purposes and functions of qualitative and quantitative data on questionnaires are different, yet complementary. The statistics from standardized items make summaries, comparisons, and generalizations quite easy and precise. The narrative comments from open-ended questions are typically meant to provide a forum for elaborations, explanations, meanings, and new ideas.

While these examples have focused on comparing quantitative and qualitative questionnaire items, the major way in which the qualitative evaluator seeks to understand the perceptions, feelings, and knowledge of people in programs is through in-depth, intensive interviewing. The chapter on interviewing will discuss ways of gathering high-quality information from people—data which reveal experiences with program activities and perspectives on program impacts from the points of view of participants, staff, and others involved in and knowledgeable about the program being evaluated.

The Aims of Observation

What people say is a major source of qualitative data, whether what they say is obtained verbally through an interview or in written form through document analysis or survey responses. There are limitations, however, to how much can be learned from what people say. To understand fully the complexities of many program situations, direct participation in and observation of the program may be the best methods.

Observational data, especially participant observation, permits the evaluator to understand a program setting to an extent not entirely possible using only the insights of others obtained through interviews. Of course, not everything can be directly observed or experienced; and participant observation is highly labor intensive and therefore a relatively expensive evaluation strategy. In a later chapter, strategies for using observational methods, including both participant and nonparticipant approaches, will be discussed at length.

A primary purpose of observational description is to take the reader of the evaluation report into the program setting that was observed. This means that observational data must have depth and detail. The data must be highly descriptive, sufficiently descriptive that the reader can understand what occurred and how it occurred. The evaluation observer becomes the surrogate eyes and ears for the reader. The descriptions must be factual, accurate, and thorough without being cluttered by irrelevant minutiae and trivia. In short, the first criterion to apply to a reported observation is the extent to which that observation permits the reader to enter the program situation observed. Evaluation data collection through observations is enormously demanding work.

Validity in qualitative methods hinges to a great extent on the skill, competence, and rigor of the evaluator because the observer *is* the instrument. Guba and Lincoln (1981) comment on this validity challenge as follows:

> Since as often as not the naturalistic inquirer is himself the instrument, changes resulting from fatigue, shifts in knowledge, and cooperation, as well as variations, resulting from differences in training, skill, and experience among different "instruments," easily occur. But this loss in rigor is more than offset by the flexibility, insight, and ability to build on tacit knowledge that is the peculiar province of the human instrument. (Guba & Lincoln, 1981, p. 113)

Integrating Observation and Interviewing Skills

Thus far the discussions of observation and interviewing have treated these two qualitative data collection techniques as separate and distinct from each other. In practice they are typically fully integrated approaches.

Becoming a skilled observer is essential for qualitative evaluation work even if the evaluator concentrates primarily on interviewing because *every face-to-face interview also involves and requires observation. The skilled interviewer is also a skilled observer,* able to read nonverbal messages, sensitive to how the interview setting can affect what is said, and carefully attuned to the nuances of the interviewer-interviewee interaction and relationship. Likewise, interviewing skills are essential for the observer because the evaluator personally visiting a program will need and want to talk with people, whether formally or informally. Participant observers gather a great deal of information through informal, naturally occurring conversations during periods of program participation.

Understanding that interviewing and observation are mutually reinforcing qualitative techniques is a bridge to understanding the major themes involved in qualitative evaluation methods. First, the qualitative evaluator must have sufficient direct, personal contact with the people and program being evaluated to understand what is happening in depth and detail. Second, the qualitative evaluator must be able to provide a meaningful context for what takes place and what people actually say. Third, the qualitative evaluator will report a great deal of pure description of people, activities, and interactions. Fourth, the evaluator will capture and report direct quotations from people, both what they say and what they write down.

The next sections further develop some of the major themes in qualitative methods.

Themes in Qualitative Methods

Naturalistic Inquiry

Qualitative designs are *naturalistic* to the extent that the evaluator does not attempt to manipulate the program or its participants for purposes of the evaluation. Evaluators engaged in naturalistic inquiry study naturally occurring activities and processes. These activities are "natural" in the sense that they are not planned and manipulated by the evaluator as would be the case in an experiment.

A naturalistic inquiry approach is particularly useful for studying variations in program implementation. What happens in a program often varies over time as participants and conditions change. Programs that are being implemented in numerous locations will manifest important differences from site to site. The nature of these variations and differences cannot be fully predicted or anticipated. By capturing whatever happens to occur, a naturalistic inquiry is open and sensitive to deviations from plans, unanticipated variations, and important idiosyncrasies of program experience.

Likewise, the experiences of program participants may vary in important ways from what staff or funders expect. A program may, and often does, have significantly different effects on different participants. There may be unanticipated impacts and unforeseen side effects. Naturalistic inquiry can capture whatever significant outcomes occur because the design is not locked into looking at only predetermined variables and outcomes.

The decision whether to employ a naturalistic inquiry or experimental approach is closely connected to the relative importance of causal questions in an evaluation. When the most important function of evaluation is to precisely measure specific, predetermined effects of a program on participants in order to make valid causal inferences, a strong case can be made for randomized experiments as "the standard against which other designs for impact evaluation are judged" (Boruch & Rindskopf, 1984, p. 121). Evaluation experiments require well-controlled settings and precise, standardized measures of program effects.

In contrast, naturalistic inquiry evaluators focus on capturing program processes, documenting variations, and exploring important individual differences between various participants' experiences and outcomes. The important distinction is between relative degrees of calculated manipulation. A naturalistic inquiry strategy is selected to describe naturally unfolding program processes and impacts. Experimental designs are selected to test the effects of controlled treatments, reduce variation in extraneous variables, and focus on a limited set of predetermined measures.

It is also important to understand that the decision to use naturalistic inquiry or an experimental approach is a *design* issue. This is a separate issue from that of what kind of data to collect (qualitative, quantitative, or some combination), although design and data alternatives are clearly related. Qualitative data can be collected in experimental designs where participants have been randomly divided into treatment and control groups. Likewise, some quantitative data may be collected in naturalistic inquiry approaches. Nevertheless, experimental designs predominantly aim for statistical analyses of quantitative data, while qualitative data are the primary focus in naturalistic inquiry. This relationship between design and measurement will be explored at greater length in Chapter 3.

Inductive Analysis

Qualitative methods are particularly oriented toward exploration, discovery, and inductive logic. An evaluation approach is inductive to the extent that the evaluator attempts to make sense of the situation without imposing pre-existing expectations on the program setting. Inductive designs begin with specific observations and build toward general patterns. Categories or dimensions of analysis emerge from open-ended observations as the evaluator comes to understand the existing program patterns.

This contrasts with the hypothetical-deductive approach of experimental designs that require the specification of main variables and the statement of specific research hypotheses *before* data collection begins. Qualitative analysis is guided not by hypotheses but by questions, issues, and a search for patterns.

Evaluation can be inductive in two ways. Within programs, an inductive approach begins with questions about the individual experiences of participants. Between programs, the inductive approach looks for unique institutional characteristics that make each setting a case unto itself. At either level, extrapolations may emerge when case materials are content analyzed, but the initial focus is on full understanding of individual cases before those unique cases are combined or aggregated. This means that evaluation findings are grounded in specific contexts. Theories that result from the findings are grounded in real-world patterns (Glaser & Strauss, 1967).

In evaluation the classic deductive approach is measuring relative attainment of predetermined clear, specific, and measurable goals. In contrast, the classic inductive approach is goal-free evaluation in which the evaluator gathers qualitative data on actual program impacts through direct observations of program activities and in-depth interviews with participants, without being limited to stated, predetermined goals. A more straightforward contrast is between close-ended questionnaires and open-ended interviews. A structured, multiple-choice questionnaire requires a deductive approach because items must be predetermined based on some criteria about what is important to measure. An open-ended interview, by way of contrast, permits the respondent to describe what is meaningful and salient without being pigeonholed into standardized categories.

In practice, these approaches are often combined. Some evaluation questions are determined deductively while others are left sufficiently open to permit inductive analyses based on direct observations. Indeed, there is often a flow from inductive approaches to find out what the important questions and variables are (exploratory work), to deductive hypothesis-testing aimed at confirming exploratory findings, then back again to inductive analysis to look for rival hypotheses and unanticipated or unmeasured factors.

Direct Contact with the Program:
Going Into the Field

Fieldwork is the central activity of qualitative evaluation methods. "Going into the field" means having direct and personal contact with people in the program in their own environments. Qualitative approaches emphasize the importance of getting close to the people and situations being studied in order to understand personally the realities and minutiae of daily program life. The evaluator gets close to the people under study through physical proximity for a period of time as well as through development of closeness in the social sense of shared experience and confidentiality.

Fieldwork involves getting one's hands dirty, participating where possible in actual program activities, and getting to know program staff and participants on a personal level. This is in sharp contrast to the style of evaluation which emphasizes detachment and distance. Such detachment and lack of personal involvement are presumed to contribute to objectivity and to reduce bias. However, qualitative evaluators question the necessity and utility of distance and detachment, assuming that without empathy and sympathetic introspection derived from personal encounters, the observer cannot fully understand human behavior. Understanding comes from trying to put oneself in the other person's shoes, from trying to discern how others think, act, and feel.

Educational evaluator Edna Shapiro (1973) studied young children in classrooms in the National Follow Through Program using both quantitative and qualitative methods. It was her closeness to the children in those classrooms that allowed her to see that important learning was occurring which was not captured by standardized tests. She observed the tension of children in the testing situation and their spontaneity in the more natural classroom setting. Had she worked solely with data collected by others or only at a distance, she would never have discovered the crucial differences in the classroom settings she studied—differences which actually allowed her to evaluate the innovative program in a meaningful and relevant way. Where standardized tests showed no differences, her direct observations documented important and significant program impacts.

Going into the field and having personal contact with program participants is not the only legitimate way to understand human behavior. For certain questions and for situations involving large groups, distance is inevitable, but for others face-to-face interaction is both necessary and desirable. The challenge is thus one of matching evaluation methods to the evaluation situation and stakeholder information needs.

In thinking about the issue of proximity to the program being evaluated, it is useful to remember that many major contributions to our understanding of the world have come from scientists' personal experiences. One finds many instances where closeness to sources of data made key insights possible—Piaget's closeness to his children, Freud's proximity to and empathy with his patients, Darwin's closeness to nature, and even Newton's intimate encounter with an apple.

In short, closeness does not make bias and loss of perspective inevitable; distance is no guarantee of objectivity. The mandate of qualitative methods is to go into the field and learn about the program firsthand.

A Holistic Perspective

Evaluators using qualitative methods strive to understand programs and situations as a whole. The evaluator searches for the totality—the unifying nature of particular settings. This holistic approach assumes that the whole is greater than the sum of its parts. It also assumes that a description and understanding of a program's social and political context is essential for overall understanding of that program.

The advantage of qualitative portrayals of programs as holistic settings is that detailed attention can be given to nuance, setting, interdependencies, complexities, idiosyncrasies, and context. John Dewey advocated this kind of holistic approach in order to reach into and understand the world of the child.

The child's life is an integral, a total one. He passes quickly and readily from one topic to another, as from one spot to another, but is not conscious of transition or break. There is no conscious isolation, hardly conscious distinction. The things that occupy him are held together by the unity of the personal and social interests which his life carries along. . . . [His] universe is fluid and fluent; its contents dissolve and reform with amazing rapidity. But after all, it is the child's own world. It has the unity and completeness of his own life. (Dewey, 1956, pp. 5-6)

Deutscher adds that despite the totality of our personal experiences as living, working human beings, in our research we have focused on parts to the virtual exclusion of wholes:

> We knew that human behavior was rarely if ever directly influenced or explained by an isolated variable; we knew that it was impossible to assume that any set of such variables was additive (with or without weighting); we knew that the complex mathematics of the interaction among any set of variables, was incomprehensible to us. In effect, although we knew they did not exist, we defined them into being. (Deutscher, 1970, p. 33)

While most evaluators would view this radical critique of variable analysis as too extreme, the reaction of many program staff to scientific research is like the reaction of Copernicus to the astronomers of his day: "With them," he observed, "it is as though an artist were to gather the hands, feet, head, and other members for his images from diverse models, each part excellently drawn, but not related to a single body, and since they in no way match each other, the result would be monster rather than man" (quoted in Kuhn, 1970, p. 83). The purpose of a holistic approach is to avoid creating a program evaluation monster of isolated, unrelated and out-of-context parts.

A Dynamic, Developmental Perspective

The qualitative-naturalistic approach to evaluation conceives of programs as dynamic and developing, with "treatments" changing in subtle but important ways as staff learn, as clients move in and out, and as conditions of delivery are altered. A primary interest of qualitative-naturalistic evaluators is describing and understanding these dynamic program processes and their holistic effects on participants so as to provide information for program improvement (*formative evaluation*).

The qualitative-naturalistic-formative approach is thus especially appropriate for programs that are developing, innovative, or changing, where the focus is on program improvement, facilitating more effective implementation, and exploring a variety of effects on participants. This can be particularly important early in the life of a program or at major points of transition.

As an innovation or program change is implemented, it frequently unfolds in a manner quite different from what was planned or conceptualized in a proposal. Once in operation, innovative programs are often changed as practitioners learn what works and what does not, as they experiment, and as they develop and change their priorities. Such conditions call for a dynamic evaluation approach that is process-oriented, capable of capturing and monitoring not only anticipated outcomes but also unanticipated consequences, treatment changes, and the larger context of program implementation and development. Qualitative methods are well suited for these challenges.

Case Studies

The depth and detail of qualitative methods typically derive from a small number of case studies, too small for confident generalizations. Cases are selected because they serve a particular evaluation purpose. Alternative ways of sampling cases for in-depth analysis will be discussed in Chapter 3.

Case studies become particularly useful where one needs to understand some particular problem or situation in great depth, and where one can identify cases rich in information   rich in the sense that a great deal can be learned from a few exemplars of the phenomenon in question. For example, a great deal can often be learned about how to improve a program by studying select dropouts, failures, or successes.

Case studies are particularly valuable when the evaluation aims to capture individual differences or unique variations from one program setting to another, or from one program experience to another. A case can be a person, an event, a program, a time period, a critical incident, or a community. Regardless of the unit of analysis, a qualitative case study seeks to describe that unit in depth, in detail, in context, and holistically. *The more a program aims at individualized outcomes, the greater the appropriateness of qualitative case methods.* The more a program emphasizes common outcomes for all participants, the greater may be the appropriateness of standardized quantitative measures of performance and change.

The Roots of Qualitative Evaluation Methods

Qualitative methods are derived most directly from the ethnographic and field study traditions of anthropology (see Pelto & Pelto, 1978) and sociology (see Bruyn, 1966). More generally, the philosophical and theoretical perspectives which undergird qualitative methods include phenomenology (see Bussis, Chittenden, & Amarel, 1973; Carini, 1975), symbolic interactionism and naturalistic behaviorism (see Denzin, 1978a, 1978b), ethnomethodology (see Garfinkel, 1967), and ecological psychology (see Barker, 1968). An integrating theme running through these perspectives is the notion that the study of human beings is fundamentally different from other scientific inquiries, for example, agricultural and natural sciences.

> Human beings can be understood in a manner that other objects of study cannot. Men have purposes and emotions, they make plans, construct cultures, and hold certain values, and their behavior is influenced by such values, plans, and purposes. In short, a human being lives in a world which has "meaning" to him, and, because his behavior has meaning, human actions are intelligible in ways that the behavior of nonhuman objects is not. The opponents of this view, on the other hand, will maintain that human behavior is to be explained in the same manner as is the behavior of other objects of nature. There are laws governing human behavior. An action is explained when it can be subsumed under some such law, and, of course, such laws are confirmed by empirical evidence. (Strike, 1972, p. 28)

The philosophical roots of qualitative methods emphasize the importance of understanding the *meanings* of human behavior and the social-cultural context of social interaction. This includes developing *empathetic* understanding based on subjective experience, and understanding the connections between personal perceptions and behavior. The qualitative perspective "in no way suggests that the researcher lacks the ability to be scientific while collecting the data. On the contrary, it merely specifies that it is crucial for validity—and, consequently, for reliability—to try to picture the empirical social world as it actually exists *to those under investigation,* rather than as the researcher imagines it to be" (Filstead, 1970, p. 4). Such field techniques as participant observation, in-depth interviewing, detailed description, and case studies typically include portrayals of the world as understood by the people studied, as well as the researcher's own understandings.

From Philosophical Controversy to
Practical Evaluation

Qualitative methods have also been the subject of considerable controversy among social scientists and evaluators. The philosophical controversies include the following issues:

- What is reality?
- Is there a single, knowable reality or only multiple, fluid perspectives on reality?
- What does it mean to know something?
- What is the nature of human experience?

The related methodological issues include:

- To what extent are human reports and observations trustworthy?
- By what criteria shall data quality be judged?
- What constitutes valid and reliable data?
- What is proof?
- How does one—or even can one—know that something caused something else?
- What's worth studying? What's worth knowing?
- What does it mean to be objective? Is objectivity possible? Is it desirable?

This book cannot resolve these issues, though the final chapter will look in greater detail at how these controversies and issues affect evaluation politics and methods decisions. At this point it is sufficient to note that qualitative methods are often quite controversial because methods choices are linked to basic philosophical questions about the nature of reality and fundamental issues about what's important to know and how best to know it.

On the practical side, however, one need not have resolved these philosophy of science problems to use qualitative methods. Nor is it necessary to be a qualitative methods purist. Qualitative data can be collected and used in conjunction with quantitative data. The beginning point for using qualitative methods is simply an interest in observing and asking questions in real-world settings.

A major challenge in evaluation is matching research methods to the nuances of particular evaluation questions and the idiosyncrasies of specific stakeholder needs. To meet this challenge evaluators need a large repertoire of research methods and techniques to use on a variety of problems. Thus an evaluator may be called on to use any and all social science research methods, including analyses of quantitative data, questionnaire results, secondary data analysis, cost-benefit and cost-effectiveness analyses, standardized tests, experimental designs, unobtrusive measures, participant observation, and in-depth interviewing. The evaluator works with stakeholders to design an evaluation that includes any and all data that will help shed light on important evaluation questions, given constraints of resources and time. Such an evaluator is committed to research designs that are relevant, meaningful, understandable, and able to produce useful results that are valid, reliable, and believable. On many occasions a variety of data collection techniques and design approaches may be used together. Multiple methods and a variety of data sources can contribute to methodological rigor. In the next chapter those evaluation situations which particularly lend themselves to the use of qualitative methods will be described and discussed.

For Further Reading

Bogdan, R., & Taylor, S. J. (1975). *Introduction to qualitative methods.* New York: John Wiley.

Cronbach, L. J. (1982). *Toward reform of program evaluation.* San Francisco: Jossey-Bass.

Denzin, N. K. (1978a). The logic of naturalistic inquiry. In N. K. Denzin (Ed.), *Sociological methods: A sourcebook.* New York: McGraw-Hill.

Filstead, W. J. (Ed.). (1970). *Qualitative methodology.* Chicago: Markham.

Guba, E. G. (1978). *Toward a methodology of naturalistic inquiry in educational evaluation* (CSE Monograph Series in Evaluation No. 8). Los Angeles: Center for the Study of Evaluation, University of California, Los Angeles.

Lincoln, Y. S., & Guba, E. G. (1985). *Naturalistic inquiry.* Newbury Park, CA: Sage.

Lofland, J. (1971). *Analyzing social settings.* Belmont, CA: Wadsworth.

Willems, E. P., & Raush, H. L. (1969) [Eds.]. *Naturalistic viewpoints in psychological research.* New York: Holt, Rinehart & Winston.

Chapter 2
When to Use Qualitative
Methods

The aim of this chapter is to suggest when it may be particularly appropriate to use qualitative methods in evaluation. Certain evaluation purposes, questions, and situations are more consonant with qualitative methods than are others. This chapter discusses those types of evaluations for which qualitative research strategies are especially powerful and appropriate.

Process Evaluations

Process evaluations are aimed at elucidating and understanding the internal dynamics of program operations. They focus on the following kinds of questions: What are the factors that come together to make this program what it is? What are the strengths and weaknesses of the program? How are clients brought into the program and how do they move through the program once they are participants? What is the nature of staff-client interactions?

Process evaluations most typically require a detailed description of program operations. Such descriptions may be based on observations and/or interviews with staff, clients, and program administrators. Many process evaluations focus on how the program is perceived by participants and by staff. The effort to generate an accurate and detailed description of program operations particularly lends itself to the use of qualitative methods.

The "process" focus in an evaluation implies an emphasis on looking at *how* a product or outcome is produced rather than looking at the product itself; that is, it is an analysis of the processes whereby a program produces the results it does. Process evaluation is developmental, descriptive, continuous, flexible, and inductive.

The process evaluator sets out to understand and document the day-to-day reality of the programs under study. The evaluator tries to unravel what is actually happening in a program in a search for major patterns and important nuances that give the program its character. A process evaluation requires sensitivity to both qualitative and quantitative change in programs throughout their development; it means becoming intimately acquainted with the details of the program. Process evaluations look not only at formal activities and anticipated outcomes, but they also investigate informal patterns and unanticipated consequences in the full context of program implementation and development. Finally, process evaluations usually include the perceptions of people close to the program about how things are going. A variety of perspectives may be sought from people with dissimilar relationships to the program—inside and outside sources.

Under what conditions are process evaluations undertaken? Process evaluations permit decision makers and information users to understand the dynamics of program operations. Such understanding allows people to decide about the extent to which the program is operating the way it is supposed to be operating. Process evaluations are particularly useful for revealing areas in which programs can be improved as well as highlighting those strengths of the program which should be preserved. Process evaluations are also useful in permitting people not intimately involved in the program—for example, external funders, public officials, and external agencies—to understand how a program operates. This permits such external persons to make more intelligent decisions about their own responsibilities with regard to such programs. Finally, process evaluations are particularly useful for dissemination and replication of programs under conditions where a program has served as a demonstration project or is considered to be a model worthy of replication at other sites.

Evaluating Individualized Outcomes

A major concern in many programs is individualization. Individualization means matching program services to the needs of individual clients. Highly individualized programs operate under the assumption that outcomes will be different for different clients. Not only will outcomes vary along specific common dimensions, but outcomes will be qualitatively different and will involve qualitatively different dimensions for different clients. Under such conditions, program staff are justifiably reluctant to generate standardized criteria and scales against which all clients are compared. They argue for documentation of the unique outcomes of individual clients rather than for measures of outcomes standardized across all clients.

There are numerous examples of such programs. Some educational approaches, for example, place a great deal of emphasis on the unique and individual needs of each child. Such programs provide a set of processes and activities for students with the full expectation that the outcomes of having engaged in those activities will be meaningfully different for different students. Thus a group of students in an open classroom may engage in some language experience that involves a field trip, dictating stories to the teachers and volunteers about that field trip, and then learning to read their stories. For some students such a process may involve learning about the mechanics of language: sentence construction, parts of speech, and verb conjugation, for example. For other students the major outcome of such a process may be learning about how to spell certain words. For other students the important outcome may be having generated an idea and conceptualized that idea based on a particular experience. For yet other students, the important outcome may have been something that was learned in the exercise or experience itself, such as knowledge about the firehouse or farm that was visited. Other students may become more articulate as a result of the dictation exercise. Still other students may have learned to read better as a result of the reading part of the exercise. The critical point is that a common process engaged in by all students can result in drastically different outcomes for different students depending on how they approach the process, what their unique needs are, and which part of the process they find most stimulating.

A similar case can be made with regard to the individualization of criminal justice, community mental health, job training, welfare, and health programs. Take, for example, the goal of increased independence among a group of clients receiving treatment in a community mental health center. It is possible to construct a test which can be administered to a large group of people measuring their relative degrees of independence. Indeed, such tests exist; these typically ask what kind of activities a person engages in and takes responsibility for, such as personal hygiene, transportation, initiatives in social interaction, food preparation, and so on. In many programs measuring such criteria in a standardized fashion provides information that program staff would like to have. However, in programs that emphasize individualization of treatment and outcomes, program staff may argue, quite justifiably, that independence has a different meaning for different people under different life conditions. Thus, for example, for one person independence may have to do with a changing family dynamic and changed relationships with parents. For another person, independence may have to do with nonfamilial relationships—that is, interactions with persons of the opposite sex, social activities, and friendships. For still other clients the dominant motif in independence may have to do with employment and economic factors. For still others it has to do with learning to live alone.

While clients or students in a program may experience a similar program process, the meaning of the outcomes for their personal lives may be quite different. What program staff want to document under such conditions is the unique meaning of the outcomes for each client. What they want and need is descriptive information about how clients' lives change over the period of treatment and following treatment. They need descriptive information about what a client's life was like upon entering treatment, about the client's response to treatment, and about what the client's life was like following treatment. Such descriptive information results in a set of individual case studies. By combining these case histories it is possible to construct an overview of the pattern of outcomes for a particular treatment facility or modality. Such clinical information is not obtained through the sole use of standardized tests and quantitative scales. Thus qualitative methods and design strategies can be particularly useful for evaluating programs which emphasize individualized client outcomes.

Case Studies

The desire to document individualized client outcomes is one major reason why case studies may be useful. There are other reasons why case studies may be helpful. Sometimes staff or funders are puzzled by particular cases—unusual successes, unusual failures, or dropouts. Detailed case studies of these extreme cases may generate particularly useful information.

In other situations, a case study approach may be indicated by the critical nature of one or a few cases. For example, if a new type of clientele enters the program—for example, clients with different backgrounds or program histories—it may be useful to gather in-depth information about these new clients and their experiences in the program. The same need for case study data may be present at the program level. A statewide or national project may spin off an innovative local program that is of special interest to decision makers, making a case study of that particular program an attractive option.

The next chapter, which is on the design of qualitative research designs, will discuss in detail sampling strategies for selecting critical cases for study. The point here is that many evaluation questions lend themselves to collection of qualitative case data.

Implementation Evaluation

It is important to know the extent to which a program is effective after it is fully implemented; but to answer that question it is first necessary to know how and the extent to which the program was actually implemented. In his important book *Social Program Implementation* (1976), editor Walter Williams concluded, "the lack of concern for implementation is currently *the* crucial impediment to improving complex operating programs, policy analysis, and experimentation in social policy areas" (Williams, 1976, p. 267).

A decision maker can use implementation information to make sure that a policy is being put into operation according to design, or to test the very feasibility of the policy. Unless one knows that a program is operating according to design, there may be little reason to expect it to provide the desired outcomes. Furthermore, until the program is implemented and a "treatment" is believed to be in operation, there may be little reason to even bother evaluating outcomes. Where outcomes are evaluated without knowledge of implementation, the results seldom provide a direction for action because the decision maker lacks information about what produced the observed outcomes (or lack of outcomes). This is the "black box" approach to evaluation.

One important way of studying program implementation is to gather detailed, descriptive information about what the program is doing in order to answer the following kinds of questions: What do clients in the program experience? What services are provided to clients? What do staff do? What is it like to be in the program? How is the program organized? Implementation evaluations tell decision makers what is going on in the program and how the program has developed.

The study of these important program implementation questions requires case data rich with the details of program content and context. Because it is impossible to anticipate in advance how programs will adapt to local conditions, needs, and interests, it is impossible to anticipate what standardized quantities could be used to capture the essence of each program's implementation. Under these evaluation conditions a strategy of naturalistic inquiry is particularly appropriate.

Describing Diversity Across Program Sites

National and statewide programs typically include a number of local sites. Implementation at the local level often involves adapting the program to local community needs and circumstances. While some basic framework of how programs should function may originate in Washington, D.C., or some state capital, it is clear that program implementation at the local level seldom follows exactly the proposed design. Instead, programs are adapted to local needs and circumstances and show considerable differences in kind—differences in content, in process, in goals, in implementation, in politics, in context, in outcomes, and in program quality. To understand these differences a holistic evaluation picture of each local site may be needed—a picture that captures each site in its own terms, not just in the limited terms of the national program which spawned it. Such a picture is important to capture the unique diversities and contrasts that mark local programs and to understand how and why programs deviate from initial plans and expectations.

Further, because program implementation is characterized by a process of adaptation to local conditions, needs, and interests, the methods used to study implementation must be open-ended, discovery oriented, and capable of describing developmental processes and program change. Qualitative methods are ideally suited to the task.

Formative Evaluation

Evaluator's Handbook, Volume 1 in the *Program Evaluation Kit*, discusses at length the differences between formative and summative evaluations. Formative evaluations are conducted for the purpose of improving programs. Summative evaluations are conducted to make basic decisions about whether a program is effective and whether it should be continued.

Formative evaluations often include a process evaluation strategy, as described earlier in this chapter. Utilizing qualitative methods, formative evaluations can be highly descriptive. They can provide depth and detail about the program's strengths and weaknesses. What's working? What's not working so well? What are the perceptions of program participants? of program staff?

Formative evaluations are particularly valuable in the early stages of a program when there is likely to be a great deal of development and change. As staff try out new approaches and adapt to client needs, a formative evaluation can provide feedback about program processes and effects on program participants. Naturalistic inquiry evaluation strategies are especially useful under these conditions to allow the evaluator to follow whatever developments turn out to be important.

Feedback given by the formative evaluator as well as actions taken as a result of formative evaluation information become part of the developmental evaluation record; that is, formative evaluators must document and describe not only program developments but also *their role* as formative evaluators in those program developments.

Finally, formative evaluations may focus on gathering descriptive information about the *quality* of program activities and outcomes, not just levels or amounts of attainment. Formative evaluations are aimed at improving program quality. Judgments about quality often require data of considerable depth and detail—qualitative data. The next section discusses further the appropriateness of qualitative methods for evaluating program quality.

Using Qualitative Methods to Evaluate Quality

There are many aspects of program operations, including implementation activities and client outcomes, that can be measured in terms of relative quantity. It makes sense to count the number of people who enter a program, the number who leave the program, and the number who receive or report some concrete benefit from the program. There are many attributes of programs, however, that do not lend themselves to counting. Even the scaling of quality attributes is an inadequate way of capturing either program quality or the effect of a program on the quality of life experienced by participants following the program.

School outcomes can be looked at both in terms of quantity of change and quality of change. Quantity of change may involve the number of books read; a score on a standardized achievement test; the number of words spelled correctly; and the number of interactions with other students, the teacher, or people of a different race. Each of these outcomes has a corresponding quality dimension which requires description rather than scaling. Thus to find out what it means to a student to have read a certain number of books is an issue of quality. How those books affected the student personally and intellectually is a question of quality. In contrast to counting the correct number of words spelled, the quality issue focuses on what spelling *means* to the student. How is spelling integrated into the student's life? How does the student think about spelling, approach spelling, feel about spelling? The answers to such questions require description of the student's perspective and situation such that the meaning of the experience for the student is recorded.

The same distinction holds with regard to programs that emphasize deinstitutionalization—for example, community mental health programs, community corrections, and community-based programs for the elderly. It is possible to count the number of people placed in the community. It is possible even to measure on standardized scales certain attributes of their lives. It is possible to have them subjectively rate various aspects and dimensions of quality of life. However, to grasp fully the meaning of a change in life for particular clients and persons it is necessary to develop a description of life quality which allows the interdependent parts of quality to be integrated into a whole.

Quality has to do with nuance, with detail, with the subtle and unique things that make a difference beyond the points on a standardized scale. Quality is what separates and falls between those points on a standardized scale. Quality descriptions provide the detail to explain what the lives of two different people are like, one of whom responded on a scale of five points that he or she had a "highly" satisfactory experience, the other of whom responded that he or she had an "extremely" satisfying experience. This is not a question of interval versus ordinal scaling, but one of meaning. What do programs mean to participants? What is the quality of their experience? Answers to such questions require detailed, in-depth, and holistic descriptions that represent people in their own terms and that get close enough to the situation being studied to understand firsthand the nuances of quality.

The failure to find statistically significant differences in comparing people on some outcome measure does *not* mean that there are no important differences among those people on those outcomes. The differences may simply be qualitative rather than quantitative. A carpenter is reported to have explained this point to William James. The carpenter, having worked for many different people, observed, "There is very little difference between one man and another; but what little there is, is very important." Those differences are differences of quality.

Quality Assurance and Quality Enhancement

Quality assurance systems involve data collection and evaluation procedures to document and support the promise made by health and mental health care providers to funding sources, including third-party insurance carriers and consumers, "that certain standards of excellence are being met. It usually involves measuring the quality of care given to individual clients in order to improve the appropriateness, adequacy, and effectiveness of care" (Lalonde, 1982, pp. 352-353). As quality assurance systems have developed, special emphasis has been placed on detecting problems, correcting deficiencies, reducing errors, and protecting individual patients. In addition, quality assurance aims to control costs of health care by preventing overutilization of services and overbilling by providers.

Important methods of quality assurance include clinical case investigations and peer reviews. All cases that fail to meet certain standards are reviewed in depth and detail. For example, patients who remain hospitalized beyond an accepted or expected period may trigger a review. A primary difference between program evaluation and quality assurance is that quality assurance focuses on individuals on a case-by-case basis while program evaluation focuses on the overall program. The concerns with unique individual cases and quality in quality assurance systems are quite consonant with qualitative methods. Quality assurance efforts have now moved beyond health care to the full spectrum of human service programs and government services (Human Services Research Institute, 1984).

Legislative Monitoring

Quality assurance is a very specific kind of monitoring focused on guaranteeing high-quality individual care. Sometimes legislators and other funders request a more general kind of program monitoring. There are many occasions when some legislative body that has mandated and appropriated funds to a new program wants to have information about whether or not the program is operating in accordance with legislative intent. Legislative intent may involve achieving certain outcomes, but more often legislative intent focuses specifically on some certain kind of delivery system being provided. The precise nature of that delivery system is often not well articulated. Thus such considerations as deinstitutionalization, decentralization, services integration, and community-based programs involve varied conceptualizations of legislative intent that do not easily lend themselves to quantitative specification. Indeed, for the evaluator to establish unilaterally some quantitative measure of deinstitutionalization that provides a global, numerical summary of the nature of program operations may hide more than it reveals.

To monitor the complexities of program implementation in the delivery of human services it can be particularly helpful to decision makers to have detailed case descriptions of how programs are operating. Such legislative monitoring would include descriptions of program facilities, outreach efforts, staff selection procedures, the nature of services offered to clients, descriptions of actual service delivery activities, and descriptions from clients about the nature of their experiences and the results of their experiences. While busy legislators cannot be expected to read in detail a large number of such histories, legislators or funders are likely to be particularly interested in the case histories of those programs that are within their own jurisdiction or legislative district, and, more generally, certain legislative staff who are particularly interested in the program can be expected to read such case histories with some care. From a political point of view, programs are more likely to be in trouble or cause trouble for legislators because they fail to follow legislative intent in implementation rather than because they fail to achieve desired outcomes.

In this case, *the purpose of legislative monitoring is to become the eyes and ears of the legislature.* This means trying to provide descriptions of programs that are sufficiently detailed and elucidating that the legislator or legislative staff can read such descriptions and have a good idea of what that program is like. Having such descriptions enables legislators to decide whether or not their own interpretations of legislative intent are being met. Such case histories may also be of considerable service to programs being monitored because the case histories permits the programs to tell their own stories in some detail. Thus, where a program has deviated from legislative intent, a case history would be expected to include information from program administrators and program staff about constraints under which the program operates and the decisions staff have made that give the program its character.

At the same time, the collection of such case histories through site visits and program monitoring need not neglect the need for more global statements about statewide patterns in programs, or even nationwide patterns. It is quite possible through content analysis to identify major patterns of program operations and outcomes for a number of separate cases. Thus qualitative methods used for legislative monitoring allow one to document common patterns across programs as well as unique developments within specific programs.

Unobtrusive Observations

Another condition under which qualitative strategies can be particularly appropriate is where an experimental design, the administration of standardized instruments, and/or the collection of quantitative data would affect program operations by being overly intrusive. Observations of program activities and informal interviews with participants sometimes can be carried out in a less obtrusive fashion than having everyone complete some test or questionnaire. Indeed, administration of such an instrument may produce artificial results or affect program operations. The instrument itself can create a reaction which, because of its intrusiveness and interference with normal program operations and client functioning, fails to reflect accurately what has been achieved in the program.

Educational researcher Edna Shapiro (1973), to her surprise, found this to be precisely the case in her study of innovative Follow Through classrooms. She found that standardized tests can bias evaluation results by imposing an obtrusive and controlled stimulus in an environment where spontaneity, creativity, and freedom of expression are valued and encouraged. Shapiro found that the results of the test measured response to a stimulus (the test) which was essentially alien to the experience of the children. Because the classrooms she studied relied substantially less on paper-and-pencil skills than traditional schools, and because student progress was monitored daily on a personal basis without the use of written examinations, student outcomes in these classrooms could not be "objectively" measured by the sudden introduction of standardized tests.

In their imaginative book on unobtrusive measuring, Webb, Campbell, Schwartz, and Sechrest (1966) discuss at length the problems of "reactive measurement effect." A basic theme of their work is that the research subjects' knowledge and awareness that they are part of a study as they complete questionnaires or tests may distort and confound the study findings. Their documentation of the sources and nature of reactivity problems in scholarly social science research makes it highly likely that such problems are magnified in evaluation research. While qualitative methods are also subject to certain reactivity problems (to be discussed in later chapters), the less formal and less obtrusive nature of qualitative strategies for conducting evaluations can sometimes serve to reduce distorting reactions to the evaluation on the part of the people being studied.

Personalizing Evaluation

One purpose of unobtrusive observations is to reduce negative reactions to being evaluated or studied. There is another way in which qualitative approaches to evaluation can reduce negative reactions and resistance to evaluation. Qualitative approaches may be perceived by program staff and program clients as more personal in nature. Programs that are based on humanistic concerns and humanistic ideologies often resist any kind of quantification because of their perceptions about the impersonal nature of numbers and scientific categorization. The issue here is not whether or not such objections are reasonable. The point is that such objections are real and that in programs where staff, funders, and/or clients hold such views, evaluations that rely on quantitative measurement may be rejected out of hand. Whether the evaluator is right or wrong to believe that quantitative methods may be most appropriate to study the effects of such programs, if the primary decision makers and information users are going to dismiss the data simply because they are quantitative, then the evaluator may find that he or she has produced an excellent evaluation that will never be used.

In evaluating such programs, then, qualitative methods can considerably enhance the utilization of evaluation findings because the data are considered to be personal. The data are perceived as more personal because they are open-ended (and therefore do not categorize people willy-nilly); the evaluator has established close contact with the program and therefore has made the evaluation more personal; and the procedures of observation and in-depth interviewing, particularly the latter, communicate respect to respondents by making *their ideas and opinions stated in their own terms* the important data source for the evaluation. Qualitative methods may also be perceived as more personal because of their inductive strategy. This means that, again, rather than imposing on the program some predetermined model or hypotheses, the program picture unfolds in a way which takes into account idiosyncrasies, uniquenesses, and complex dynamics. Finally, qualitative methods may be perceived as more humanistic and personal simply by avoiding numbers.

Responsive Evaluation

Robert Stake's "responsive approach to evaluation" (1975) places particular emphasis on the importance of personalizing and humanizing the evaluation process. Being responsive requires having face-to-face contact with people in the program and learning firsthand about stakeholders' concerns.

> To do a responsive evaluation, the evaluator conceives of a plan of observations and negotiations. He arranges for various persons to observe the program, and with their help prepared brief narratives, portrayals, product displays, graphs, etc. He finds out what is of value to his audiences, and gathers expressions of worth from various individuals whose points of view differ. Of course, he checks the quality of his records: he gets program personnel to react to the accuracy of his portrayals; and audience members to react to the relevance of his findings. He does most of this informally— iterating and keeping a record of action and reaction. (Stake, 1975, p. 14)

Guba and Lincoln (1981) have integrated naturalistic inquiry and responsive evaluation into an overall framework for improving the usefulness of evaluation results. The openness of naturalistic inquiry permits the evaluator to be especially sensitive to the differing perspectives of various stakeholders. This sensitivity allows the evaluator to collect data and report findings with those differing perspectives clearly in mind. Responsive evaluation includes the following primary emphases:

(1) identifying issues and concerns based on direct, face-to-face contact with people in and around the program;

(2) using program documents to further identify important issues;

(3) direct, personal observation of program activities *before* formally designing the evaluation, in order to increase the evaluator's understanding of what is important in the program and what can/should be evaluated;

(4) designing the evaluation based on issues that emerged in the preceding three steps, with the design to include continuing direct qualitative observations in the naturalistic program setting;

(5) reporting information in direct, personal contact through themes and portrayals that are easily understandable and rich with description; and

(6) matching information reports and reporting formats to specific audiences with different reports and different formats for different audiences.

Goal-Free Evaluation

Program evaluation has traditionally meant measuring goal attainment, based on a carefully prespecified set of measurable goals. In contrast to this common approach to evaluation, philosopher-evaluator Michael Scriven (1972a, 1972b) has proposed the idea of "goal-free evaluation." Goal-free evaluation means gathering data directly on program effects and effectiveness without being constrained by a narrow focus on stated goals. Goal-free evaluation lends itself particularly to qualitative methods because goal-free evaluation relies heavily on description and direct experience with the program. Moreover, and in particular, goal-free evaluation requires the evaluator to suspend judgment about what it is the program is trying to do and to focus instead on finding out what it is that actually happens in the program and as a result of the program. The evaluator thus can be open to whatever data emerge from the phenomena of the program.

There are four reasons for doing goal-free evaluation: (1) to avoid the risk of narrowly studying stated program objectives and thereby missing important unanticipated outcomes; (2) to remove the negative connotations attached to the discovery of unanticipated effects ("The whole language of 'side-effect' or 'secondary-effect' or even 'unanticipated effect' tended to be a put-down of what might well be the crucial achievement, especially in terms of new priorities"; Scriven, 1972a, pp. 1-2); (3) to eliminate the perceptual biases introduced into an evaluation by knowledge of goals; and (4) to maintain evaluator objectivity and independence through goal-free conditions.

Goal-free evaluation, in its search for "actual effects," is an inductive and holistic strategy aimed at countering the logical-deductive limitations inherent in the usual quantitative goals-based approach to evaluation. It is important to note, however, that goal-free evaluations can employ both quantitative and qualitative methods. Moreover, Scriven has proposed that goal-free evaluations might be conducted along with goals-based evaluations, but with separate evaluators using each approach to maximize its strengths and minimize its weaknesses. (For a more detailed discussion of goal-free evaluation, and critiques of this idea, see Alkin, 1972; Patton, 1986).

State-of-the-Art Considerations:
Lack of Proven Quantitative Instrumentation

Another reason for gathering qualitative data in an evaluation is that for particular variables of interest no acceptable, valid, and reliable quantitative measures exist. The extent to which one believes that quantitative measures in a particular instance and for a particular variable are useful, valid, and reliable is a matter of judgment. The state of the art in social science measurement is such that a number of desirable social and psychological measures still elude precise measurement. Where rigorous measuring instruments have not been carefully developed, it is often more appropriate to gather descriptive information about what happens in a social program than to use some scale which has the merit of being quantitative but whose validity and reliability are suspect.

Creativity is a prime example. While there are some instruments that purport to measure creativity, the applicability of those instruments in diverse situations is at least open to question. Thus a program attempting to make students or clients more creative might do better to document in detail the activities, behaviors, thoughts, and feelings of participants rather than to administer some instrument. Interested decision makers or information users can then inspect and judge documentation of this kind to form their own interpretations of the extent to which creativity was exhibited by the products produced, activities undertaken, or statements made by participants.

Exploratory Evaluation Research and Evaluability Assessment

Another state-of-the-art consideration in deciding whether to use qualitative methods is the extent to which initial data collection is to be considered exploratory. The purpose of exploratory data collection is to understand enough about what is happening in the program and what outcomes may be important to then identify key variables that may be operationalized quantitatively. Exploratory research relies on naturalistic inquiry, the collection of qualitative data, and inductive analysis because sufficient information is not available to permit the use of quantitative measures and experimental designs. These come later, as the payoff of the exploratory research. This kind of exploratory evaluation data collection is sometimes referred to as "pre-evaluation" work in that it occurs before the formal, official evaluation using quantitative instruments for summative purposes.

A related idea is "evaluability assessment," which involves informal, qualitative data collection to determine if the program is ready for systematic, quantitative evaluation. An evaluability assessment involves making sure that the program "treatment" is clearly identifiable and consistent, that outcomes are clear, specific, and measurable, and that a design can be implemented which relates the treatment to expected outcomes. Thus, in this instance, qualitative approaches are used to design a quantitative, experimental evaluation (Rutman, 1980; Wholey, 1979).

Adding Depth, Detail, and Meaning to Quantitative Analyses

At the opposite end of the continuum from exploratory research is the use of qualitative methods to add depth and detail to quantitative studies where the statistical results indicate global patterns generalizable across settings or populations. For example, when a large-scale survey has revealed certain marked and significant response patterns, it is often helpful to fill out the meaning of those patterns through in-depth study using qualitative methods. The quantitative data identify areas of focus; the qualitative data give substance to those areas of focus.

What did people really mean when they marked that answer on the questionnaire? What elaborations can they provide of their responses? How do the various dimensions of analysis fit together as a whole in the program? Follow-up interviews with a subsample of respondents can provide meaningful additional detail to help make sense out of and interpret survey results. Qualitative data can put flesh on the bones of quantitative results, bringing the results to life through in-depth case elaborations.

Breaking the Routine: Generating New Insights

There is another sense in which qualitative methods provide a real and useful option in program evaluation. Programs that have established ongoing evaluation systems or management information approaches may have become lulled into a routine of producing statistical tables that are no longer studied with any care. Inertia and boredom can seriously reduce the usefulness of program evaluation results. After program staff or other decision makers have seen the same statistical results used in the same kinds of statistical tables year after year, those results can begin to have a numbing effect. Even though the implications of those results may vary somewhat from year to year, the very format used to report the data can reduce the impact of the results.

It is also worth noting that evaluators can settle into routines inertia. Evaluators who have been using the same methods over and over have lost the cutting edge of their own creativity.

Under these circumstances it may be useful to introduce qualitative methods as a new approach to evaluation. The purpose, in part, is to attract renewed interest in and attention to the evaluation findings and the evaluation process. At the same time, changing the method may produce new insights or at least force people to deal with the old insights in a new way. Of course, collection of qualitative data can also become routine. Programs of humanistic ideology and/or programs with an emphasis on individualization may find that the collection of qualitative data has become a routine and that new insights can be gained through even the temporary use of some quantitative measures.

Given the ease with which human beings and social systems can be carried along by inertia and routine, evaluators who want their results to make a difference need to find creative ways to get people to deal with issues of program effectiveness. Exploring methodological variations may be one such approach.

Grounded Theory and Program Evaluation

Evaluation research, particularly at the local program level, has been largely nontheoretical—both in conception and in reporting findings. Evaluation research often ignores theoretical issues altogether. Evaluators are accused of being technicians who simply collect data without regard to the theoretical relevance of possible empirical generalizations. Certainly, pure outcomes evaluations are nontheoretical. Moreover, in many cases decision makers need and want specific data relevant to narrow, technical issues that are helpful in monitoring or fine-tuning program operations.

However, evaluation research is by no means inherently nontheoretical. It can be theoretical in the usual scientific sense that deductive, logical systems are constructed to model causal linkages among general variables (Hage, 1972).

By way of contrast to logical, deductive theory construction, a grounded theory approach to evaluation research is inductive, pragmatic, and highly concrete. The evaluator's task is to generate program theory from holistic data gathered through naturalistic inquiry for the purpose of helping program staff and decision makers understand how the program functions, why it functions as it does, and the ways in which the impacts/consequences/outcomes of the program flow from program activities. Program staff and other program decision makers can use such grounded theory to *reality-test* their own theories of programmatic action, program effects, and the relationship between action and effects. Such grounded theory can serve to take decision makers *into the empirical world* so that they can discover whether what they think to be the nature of the empirical world is actually the case.

Grounded theory can provide relevant information which is useful to program staff and other decision makers in their efforts to understand and improve their programs. Grounded evaluation theory would be particularly useful in considerations of whether a program should be replicated in other settings and how such replication might occur. Thus grounded evaluation theory would be a particularly important product of the evaluation of demonstration programs.

Guiding Questions for Determining
When Qualitative Methods
Are Appropriate for Program Evaluation

Qualitative methods are not appropriate for every evaluation situation or for the study of all evaluation questions. This chapter has reviewed some situations and questions for which qualitative methods are particularly appropriate. This is by no means an exhaustive list of conditions under which qualitative research strategies can be useful. The various possibilities presented in this chapter are simply meant to demonstrate some of the many ways in which qualitative methods can contribute to evaluation. The following is a checklist of questions which can be used to help decide if qualitative methods are an appropriate evaluation strategy. If the answer to any of the questions is yes, then the collection of some qualitative data is likely to be appropriate.

Qualitative Evaluation Checklist

(1) Does the program emphasize *individualized outcomes,*—that is, are different participants expected to be affected in qualitatively different ways? And is there a need or desire to describe and evaluate these individualized client outcomes?

(2) Are decision makers interested in elucidating and understanding the internal dynamics of programs—program strengths, program weaknesses, and overall *program processes*?

(3) Is detailed, in-depth information needed about *certain client cases or program sites,* for example, particularly successful cases, unusual

failures, or critically important cases for programmatic, financial, or political reasons?

(4) Is there interest in *focusing on the diversity* among, idiosyncrasies of, and unique qualities exhibited by individual clients and programs (as opposed to comparing all clients or programs on standardized, uniform measures)?

(5) Is information needed about the details of *program implementation:* What do clients in the program experience? What services are provided to clients? How is the program organized? What do staff do? Do decision makers need to know what is going on in the program and how it has developed?

(6) Are program staff and other stakeholders interested in the collection of detailed, descriptive information about the program for the purpose of improving the program (i.e., is there interest in *formative evaluation*)?

(7) Is there a need for information about the nuances of *program quality*— descriptive information about the quality of program activities and outcomes, not just levels, amounts, or quantities of program activity and outcomes?

(8) Does the program need a case-specific *quality assurance* system?

(9) Are legislators or other decision makers or funders interested in having evaluators conduct *program site visits* so that the evaluators can be the surrogate eyes and ears for decision makers who are too busy to make such site visits themselves and who lack the observing and listening skills of trained evaluators? Is *legislative monitoring* needed on a case basis?

(10) Is the obtrusiveness of evaluation a concern? Will the administration of standardized measuring instruments (questionnaires and tests) be overly obtrusive in contrast to data-gathering through natural observations and open-ended interviews? Will the collection of qualitative data generate less reactivity among participants than the collection of quantitative data? Is there a need for *unobtrusive observations*?

(11) Is there a need and desire to *personalize the evaluation process* by using research methods that emphasize personal, face-to-face contact with the program—methods that may be perceived as "humanistic" and personal because they do not label and number the participants, and feel natural, informal, and understandable to participants?

(12) Is a *responsive evaluation* approach appropriate—that is, an approach that is especially sensitive to collecting descriptive data and reporting information in terms of differing stakeholder perspectives based on direct, personal contact with those different stakeholders?

(13) Are the goals of the program vague, general, and nonspecific, indicating the possible advantage of a *goal-free evaluation* approach that would gather information about what effects the program is actually having rather than measure goal attainment?

(14) Is there the possibility that the program may be affecting clients or participants in unanticipated ways and/or having unexpected side effects, indicating the need for a method of inquiry that can *discover effects* beyond those formally stated as desirable by program staff (again, an indication of the need for some form of goal-free evaluation)?

(15) Is there a *lack of proven quantitative instrumentation* for important program outcomes? Is the state of measurement science such that no valid, reliable, and believable standardized instrument is available or readily capable of being developed to measure quantitatively the particular program outcomes for which data are needed?

(16) Is the evaluation *exploratory*? Is the program at a *pre-evaluation* stage, where goals and program content are still being developed?

(17) Is an *evaluability assessment* needed to determine a summative evaluation design?

(18) Is there a need to *add depth, detail, and meaning to statistical findings* or survey generalizations?

(19) Has the collection of quantitative evaluation data become so routine that no one pays much attention to the results anymore, suggesting a possible need to *break the old routine* and use new methods to generate new insights about the program?

(20) Is there a need to *develop a program theory* grounded in observations of program activities and impacts, and the relationship between treatment and outcomes?

On Using the Qualitative Evaluation Checklist

This evaluation version of the "20 questions" game demonstrates the wide variety of situations in which qualitative methods can be used. Matching research methods to evaluation questions is a complex, creative process. The above questions are meant to stimulate and guide in that process; they are not a mechanical tool for making routine decisions. The next chapter discusses some of the concrete and practical research design issues that must be addressed in using qualitative methods.

For Further Reading

Alkin, M. C. (with Burry, J.). (1985). *A guide for evaluation decision makers.* Newbury Park, CA: Sage.

Patton, M. Q. (1986). *Utilization-focused evaluation.* Newbury Park, CA: Sage.
Stake, R. E. (1975). *Evaluating the arts in education: A responsive approach.* Columbus, OH: Charles E. Merrill.
Walker, R. (Ed.). (1985). *Applied qualitative research.* Brookfield, VT: Gower.
Weiss, C. (1972). *Evaluation research.* Englewood Cliffs, NJ: Prentice-Hall.

Chapter 3
Designing Qualitative
Evaluations

Distinguishing Conceptual from Technical Issues

The process of planning an evaluation involves attention to two kinds of issues: conceptual issues and technical issues. Conceptual issues focus on how the people involved *think about* the evaluation and include the following questions:

- Who are the primary stakeholders for the evaluation?
- What is the purpose of the evaluation?
- What approach, model, or framework will be used to provide direction for the evaluation?
- What are the primary evaluation questions or issues?
- What political considerations should be taken into account?
- By what standards and criteria will the evaluation be judged?
- What resources are available for the evaluation?

These are questions which cannot be answered by evaluators and methodologists alone. As described in the *Evaluator's Handbook* and *How to Focus an Evaluation* (Volumes 1 and 2 of the *Program Evaluation Kit*), arriving at answers to conceptual issues involves negotiation among interested participants in the evaluation: stakeholders, decision makers, and information users—including funders, staff, administrators, clients, and policymakers. The evaluator may facilitate these negotiations, or be one of the stakeholders in the negotiation process, but the evaluator ought not unilaterally dictate the answers to conceptual questions. To do so is to risk short-circuiting the process of building the political and conceptual foundation for the evaluation, which is critical to the evaluation's credibility and use.

The process of building both support for and an understanding of the evaluation is important regardless of whether the technical design is quantitative or qualitative. Since this book is concerned primarily with technical designs using qualitative methods we shall not deal further with the process of conceptualizing the overall evaluation. However, it is important to emphasize that the technical and methodological issues in evaluation are best addressed in the context of conceptual, political, and utility considerations. For additional detailed discussion of how to work with stakeholders to negotiate a credible evaluation framework aimed at high-level use of the evaluation see Patton (1986) or Alkin (1985).

Technical Design Issues

The technical design is a plan for data collection and analysis. The technical design answers the following questions:

- What will be the method(s) of inquiry?
- What will be the primary unit(s) of analysis?
- What will be the sampling strategy?
- What comparisons, if any, will be made?
- What kinds of data will be collected? From whom? When? Using what instruments?
- How will the quality and accuracy of the data be ensured? What level and type of accuracy is needed?
- How will concerns about validity and reliability be addressed?
- What kind(s) of analysis will be conducted?
- What kind(s) of statements and findings will result from the analysis?

This chapter will consider some design alternatives and strategies using qualitative methods. It is neither possible nor desirable to write a qualitative evaluation design cookbook. As this chapter will illustrate, there are a large variety of options possible depending on the purpose, nature, and questions of a particular evaluation. Thus the technical design grows out of and is matched to the conceptual direction of the evaluation. In determining both conceptual direction and technical design, alternative strategies and tradeoffs will need to be considered.

Strategies and tradeoffs—these two themes go together. A discussion of design strategies and tradeoffs is necessitated by the fact that *there are no perfect research designs*. There are always tradeoffs. These tradeoffs are necessitated by limited resources, limited time, political considerations, and limits in the human ability to grasp the complex nature of social reality.

The very first tradeoffs come in framing the evaluation issues or questions to be studied. The problem here is to determine the extent to which it is desirable to study one or a few questions in great depth or to study many questions, but in less depth. This is what Guba (1978) calls the "boundary problem" in naturalistic inquiry studies. Discussion of this problem will illustrate the relationship between conceptual issues and technical design issues. We shall then consider other technical design alternatives and qualitative sampling strategies. First, let us consider the breadth versus depth tradeoff in evaluation.

Breadth Versus Depth Tradeoff

Deciding what information and how much data to gather in an evaluation involves in part considering the relative merits of breadth versus depth. Getting more data usually takes longer and costs more, but getting less data usually reduces confidence in the findings. Studying a narrow question or very specific problem in great depth may produce very clear results but leaves other important issues and problems unexamined. On the other hand, gathering information on a large variety of issues and problems may leave the evaluation unfocused, and may result in knowing a little about a lot of things but nothing in sufficient depth to permit confident action.

The emphasis in qualitative methods is on *depth and detail*: in-depth interviews, detailed descriptions, and thorough case studies. Still, depth and detail are always relative: How much depth? How much detail? Thus in the early part of the evaluation some boundaries must be set on data collection. Should all parts of the program be studied or only certain parts? Should all clients be studied or only some subset of clients? Should the evaluator aim at describing all program processes or is there reason to examine only certain selected processes in depth? Should all outcomes be examined or should the evaluation focus on the attainment of only certain outcomes of particular interest and importance? Or of interest to only certain stakeholders?

Establishing focus and priorities can be quite difficult at the beginning of the evaluation. Once a group of decision makers and information users begin to take seriously the notion that they can learn from the collection and analysis of evaluative information, they soon find that there are lots of things they would like to know. The evaluator's role is to help primary stakeholders move from a rather extensive list of potential questions to a much shorter list of realistically possible questions, and finally to a focused list of essential and necessary questions.

An example of variations in evaluation focus may help illustrate the kinds of tradeoffs involved. Suppose that a group of educators is interested in studying how an early childhood program affects the social development of preschool-age children. They want to know how the interaction of children with others in the program contributes to the development of social skills. They believe that those social skills will be different for different children, and they are unsure of the range of social interactions that may occur, so they are interested in a *descriptive evaluation* that will explore variations in experience and capture a range of individualized outcomes.

There are several ways in which this evaluation situation leads in a qualitative direction: (1) the interest in *descriptive* data; (2) the focus on interactions and process; (3) the exploratory nature of the problem; (4) the concern with individualized experiences and outcomes—different things happening to different children with varying results; and (5) uncertainty about what interactions or variables may be most important, a clue that an inductive, naturalistic strategy may be appropriate. The conceptualization of the problem suggests a qualitative technical design.

Still, there are tradeoffs in determining the final focus. It is clear that any given child has social interactions with a great many peers and adults. The problem in focusing this evaluation is to determine how much of the social reality experienced by children should be described. A narrowly focused evaluation might involve only one particular set of interactions between teacher and children. Broadening the scope somewhat, one might decide to look at only those interactions that occur in the classroom, thereby increasing the scope of the study to include interactions not only between teacher and child, but also among peers in the classroom and between any volunteers or visitors to the classroom and the children. Broadening the scope of the evaluation still more, one might look at all of the social relationships that children experience in this preschool program; this would involve moving beyond the classroom to look at interactions with other personnel in the program—for example, social workers, counselors, special subject teachers, health workers, the custodian, and/or school administrative staff. Broadening the scope of the study still further, the stakeholders might decide that it is important to look at the social relationships children experience at home as well as in school in order to understand how children experience those settings differently, and therefore to better understand the unique effects of the early childhood program. In this case the design would include gathering data about interactions with parents, siblings, and other people in the home. Finally, one might look at the social relationships experienced throughout the full range of societal contacts that children have, including church, clubs, and neighborhood playmates to increase the comparative breadth of the analysis.

All of these are potentially important evaluation issues if one is attempting to increase the effectiveness of an early childhood educational program in developing socially competent children. Suppose now that we have a set amount of resources—for example, $25,000—to conduct the study. We also have limited time—say, three months. At some level, any of these evaluation endeavors could be undertaken for $25,000 in three months. It is immediately clear, however, that there are tradeoffs between breadth and depth. A highly focused evaluation question such as describing the socially oriented interactions between a teacher and select children could consume the entire amount of our resources and allow us to investigate the problem in some depth. On the other hand, we might attempt to look at all social relationships that children experience but to look at each of them in a relatively cursory way, in order, perhaps, to explore which of those relationships is primary. (If social relationships within the program appear to have very little impact on social development in comparison to relationships outside the program, decision makers could use that information to decide whether the preschool program ought to be redesigned to have greater impact on social development or if the program should forget about trying to directly affect social development at all.)

The tradeoffs involved are the classic tradeoffs between breadth and depth. There is no easy or right design answer. The exploratory nature of the problem suggests the desirability of breadth, but the concern with describing individualized experiences and outcomes points to a need for depth and detail. The final design emerges from discussing alternatives and deciding on the most sensible priorities given the situation, the stakeholders, and the potential for generating really useful and meaningful information.

How Deep Is Deep?

Central themes in qualitative methods are the emphasis on depth and detail. While quantitative methods (for example, questionnaire surveys) cover relatively large samples with relatively few questions, qualitative approaches aim at depth of information from relatively few cases. But, as the preceding example of the preschool program illustrated, depth is a relative notion.

There are no rules that tell evaluators how much depth and detail to strive for with qualitative methods. The breadth versus depth tradeoff is applicable not only in comparing quantitative and qualitative methods; the same tradeoff applies within either quantitative or qualitative methods. Consider the problem of how deep to go in interviewing.

The human relations specialists tell us that we can never fully understand the experience of another person. The methodological question, then, is how much time and effort we are willing to invest—and able to invest—in trying to increase our understanding about any single person's experience. Open-ended interviewing can take a great deal of time and produce volumes of narrative data. In a North Dakota evaluation of an innovative educational program we developed an open-ended interview of 20 questions for children in grades one to eight. Those questions consisted of items such as "What do you like most about school?" and "What don't you like about school?" The interviews took between half an hour and two hours depending on how articulate students were and how old they were. It would certainly have been possible to have longer interviews. Indeed, I have conducted in-depth interviews with people that ran ten to twelve hours over a few days. On the other hand, one can always ask fewer questions, make the interviews shorter, but then obtain less depth.

To illustrate this tradeoff between breadth and depth in sampling human behavior, let us consider the full range of possibilities. It is possible (and indeed it has been done) to study a single individual over an extended period of time—for example an in-depth study of the life of one child. This necessitates attempting to gather detailed information about every important occurrence in that child's life. With a more limited evaluation question we might study several children during a shorter period of time. With still a more limited focus, perhaps an interview of a half-hour, we could interview yet a larger number of children on a smaller number of issues. The extreme case would be to spend all of our resources and time asking a single question of as many children as we could interview given available time and resources.

There is no rule of thumb that tells an evaluator precisely how to focus an evaluation question or how much depth to seek. The extent to which data collection is broad or narrow depends on the resources available, the time available, and the needs of decision makers. In brief, these are not choices between good and bad, but choices among alternatives, all of which have merit.

It's relatively easy to generate a great deal of information with sophisticated evaluations made possible by abundant resources. It's also relatively easy to design an extremely simple evaluation with very limited resources, one that generates a minimum amount of straight-forward information. What is more difficult is to generate a great deal of really useful information with scarce resources. The latter challenge seems also to be the most typical.

Units of Analysis

The technical evaluation design specifies the unit or units of analysis to be studied. Decisions about samples—both sample size and sampling strategies—depend on prior decisions about the appropriate unit of analysis to study. Sometimes individual people—program participants, clients, or students—are the unit of analysis. This means that the primary focus of data collection will be on what is happening to individuals in the program.

Focusing on and comparing groups of people involve different units of analysis. Small groups, families, subcultures, formal organizations, agencies, and communities all constitute different units and levels of analysis. One may be interested in comparing demographic groups (males compared with females, whites compared with blacks) or programmatic groups (dropouts versus people who complete the program, people who do well versus people who do poorly, people who experience group therapy versus people who experience individual therapy). One or more groups are selected as the unit of analysis when there is some important characteristic that separates people into groups and that has important implications for the program.

The different units of analysis are not mutually exclusive. But each unit of analysis implies a different kind of data collection, a different focus for the analysis of data, and a different level at which statements about findings and conclusions would be made. Neighborhoods can be units of analysis, as can communities, cities, states, and even nations in the case of international programs.

A different way of conceptualizing the unit of analysis involves focusing on different parts of a program. Different classrooms within a school might be studied so that the classroom becomes the unit of analysis. Outpatient and inpatient programs in a medical facility might be studied. The intake part of a program might be studied separately from the service delivery part of a program, each as a discrete unit of analysis.

Entire programs can become the unit of analysis. In state and national programs where there are a number of local sites the appropriate unit of analysis may be local projects. The focus in this case would be on variations among projects more than on variations among individuals within programs.

In qualitative evaluations units of analysis may also be particular kinds of events, occurrences, or incidents. For example, a quality assurance effort in a physical or mental health program might focus only on those critical incidents in which a patient fails to receive expected or desirable treatment. A criminal justice evaluation could focus on violent events or instances in which juveniles run away from treatment. One of the strengths of qualitative analysis is looking at program units holistically. This means doing more than aggregating data from individuals to get overall program results. When a program, group, or community is the unit of analysis, qualitative methods involve observations and description focused directly on that unit.

The key factor in selecting and making decisions about the appropriate unit of analysis is to decide what unit it is that you want to be able to say something about at the end of the evaluation. At what level do decision makers really need information? Do they want information about the different experiences of individuals in programs or do they want to know about variations in program processes at different sites? These are differences in nuance. The decision makers will typically be unable to say to the evaluator, "The unit of analysis we want to study is . . . ." The evaluator must be able to hear the real issues involved in stakeholders' questions and translate those issues into the appropriate unit of analysis, then check out that translation with the stakeholders.

Choosing a Sample:
The Logic of Purposeful Sampling

The logic of purposeful sampling in qualitative methods is quite different from the logic of probabilistic sampling in statistics. The power of statistical sampling depends on selecting a truly random and representative sample which will permit confident generalization from the sample to a larger population. The power of purposeful sampling lies in selecting *information-rich cases* for study in depth. Information-rich cases are those from which one can learn a great deal about issues of central importance to the purpose of the evaluation, thus the term "purposeful" sampling. For example, if the purpose of the evaluation is to increase the effectiveness of a program in reaching lower socio-economic groups, one may learn a great deal more by focusing in depth on understanding the needs, interests, and incentives of a small number of carefully selected poor families than gathering a little information from a large, statistically significant sample.

There are several different strategies for purposefully selecting information-rich cases. The logic of each strategy serves a particular evaluation purpose.

(1) Extreme or deviant case sampling. This approach focuses on cases that are rich in information because they are unusual or special in some way. Unusual or special cases may be particularly troublesome or especially enlightening, such as outstanding successes or notable failures. If, for example, the evaluation was aimed at gathering data to help a program reach more clients, one might compare a few project sites with long waiting lists to those with short waiting lists. If staff morale was an issue, one might study and compare high morale programs to low morale programs.

The logic of extreme case sampling is that lessons may be learned about unusual conditions or extreme outcomes which are relevant to improving more typical programs. Let's suppose that we are interested in studying a national program with hundreds of local sites. We know that many programs are operating reasonably well, even quite well, and that other programs verge on being disasters. We also know that most programs are doing "okay." This information comes from knowledgeable sources who have made site visits to enough programs to have a basic idea about how they vary. The question is, How to sample programs for the study? If one wanted to document precisely the natural variation among programs, a random sample would be appropriate, preferably a random sample of sufficient size to be truly representative of and permit generalizations to the total population of programs. However, some information is already available on what program variation is like. The question of more immediate interest may concern *extreme cases.* With limited resources and limited time an evaluator might learn more by intensively studying one or more examples of really poor programs and one or more examples of really excellent programs. The evaluation focus, then, becomes a question of understanding what conditions programs get into trouble and under what conditions programs exemplify excellence. It is not even necessary to randomly sample poor programs or excellent programs. The policymakers and stakeholders involved in the study think through *the cases from which they could learn the most* and are the cases that are selected for study.

In a single program the same strategy may apply. Instead of studying some representative sample of people in the setting, the evaluator may focus on studying and understanding selected cases of special interest, for example, unexpected dropouts or outstanding successes. In many instances more can be learned from intensively studying extreme or unusual cases than can be learned from statistical depictions of what the average case is like. In other evaluations detailed information about special cases can be used to supplement statistical data about the normal distribution of participants.

(2) Maximum variation sampling. This strategy for purposeful sampling aims at capturing and describing the central themes or principal outcomes that cut across a great deal of participant or program variation. For small samples a great deal of heterogeneity can be a problem because individual cases are so different from each other. The maximum variation sampling strategy turns that apparent weakness into a strength by applying the following logic: Any common patterns that emerge from great variation are of particular interest and value in capturing the core experiences and central, shared aspects or impacts of a program.

How does one maximize variation in a small sample? One begins by selecting diverse characteristics for constructing the sample. Suppose a statewide program has project sites spread around the state, some in rural areas, some in urban areas, and some in suburban areas. The evaluation lacks sufficient resources to select randomly a sufficient sample of project sites to generalize to the state. The evaluator can at least be sure that the geographical variation among sites is represented in the study.

When selecting a small sample of great diversity, the data collection and analysis will yield two kinds of findings: (1) high-quality, detailed descriptions of each case which are useful for documenting uniquenesses, and (2) important shared patterns which cut across cases and which derive their significance from having emerged out of heterogeneity. The same strategy can be used within a single program in selecting individuals for study. By including in the sample individuals the evaluator determines have had quite different experiences, it is possible to describe more thoroughly the variation in the group and to understand variations in experiences, while also investigating core elements and shared outcomes. The evaluator using a *maximum variation sampling strategy* would not be attempting to generalize findings to all people or all groups, but rather looking for information that elucidates programmatic variation and significant common patterns within that variation.

(3) Homogeneous samples. In direct contrast to maximum variation sampling is the strategy of picking a small homogeneous sample. The purpose here is to describe some particular subgroup in depth. A program which has many different kinds of participants may need in-depth information about a particular subgroup. For example, a parent education program which involves many different kinds of parents may focus a qualitative evaluation on the experiences of single-parent female heads of household because that is a particularly difficult group to reach and hold in the program.

Focus group interviews are typically based on homogeneous groups. Focus group interviews involve conducting open-ended interviews with groups of five to eight people on specially targeted or focused issues. The use of focus groups in evaluation will be discussed at greater length in the chapter on interviewing. The point here is that sampling for focus groups typically involves bringing together people of similar backgrounds and experiences to participate in a group interview about major program evaluation issues which affect them.

(4) Typical case sampling. In describing a program or its participants to people not familiar with the program it can be helpful to provide a qualitative profile of one or more "typical" cases. These cases are selected with the cooperation of key informants, such as program staff or knowledgeable participants, who can help identify what is typical. It is also possible to select typical cases from survey data, a demographic analysis of averages, or other programmatic data that provide a normal distribution of characteristics from which to identify "average" examples. Keep in mind that a qualitative profile of one or more typical cases is presented in order to describe and illustrate to those unfamiliar with the program what is typical—not to make generalized statements about the experiences of all participants.

(5) Critical case sampling. Another strategy for selecting purposeful samples is to look for *critical* cases. Critical cases are those that can make a point quite dramatically or are, for some reason, particularly important in the scheme of things. A clue to the existence of a critical case is a statement to the effect that "if it happens there, it will happen anywhere," or vice versa, "if it doesn't happen there, it won't happen anywhere." In this instance the data-gathering focused on understanding what is happening in that critical case. Another clue to the existence of a critical case is a key informant observation to the effect that "if that group is having problems then we can be sure all the groups are having problems." Looking for the critical case is particularly important where resources may limit the evaluation to the study of only a single site. Under such conditions it makes strategic sense to pick the site that would yield the most information and have the greatest impact in the development of knowledge.

While studying one or a few critical cases does not technically permit broad generalizations to all possible cases, logical generalizations can often be made from the weight of evidence produced in studying a single, critical case. Physics provides a good example of such a critical case. In Galileo's study of gravity he wanted to find out if the weight of an object affected the rate of speed at which it would fall. Rather than randomly sampling objects of different weights in order to generalize to all objects in the world, he selected a critical case—the feather. If in a vacuum, as he demonstrated, a feather fell at the same rate as some heavier object (a coin) then he could logically generalize from this one critical case to all objects. His findings were enormously useful *and* credible.

There are many comparable critical cases in social science research— if one is creative in looking for them. For example, suppose national policymakers want to get local communities involved in making decisions about how their local program will be run, but they are not sure that the communities will understand the complex regulations governing their involvement. The first critical case is to evaluate the regulations in a community of well-educated citizens; if they cannot understand them, less-educated folks are sure to find the regulations incomprehensible. Or, conversely, one might consider the critical case to be a community consisting of people with quite low levels of education; "if they can understand the regulations, anyone can."

Identification of critical cases depends on recognition of the key dimensions that make for a critical case. A critical case might be indicated by the financial state of a program; a program with particularly high or particularly low cost-per-client ratios might suggest a critical case. A critical case might come from a particularly difficult program location. If the funders of a new program are worried about recruiting clients or participants into a program, it may make sense to study the site where resistance to the program is expected to be greatest to provide the most rigorous test of the possibility of program recruitment. If the program works in that site, "it could work anywhere."

(6) Snowball or chain sampling. This is an approach for locating information-rich key informants or critical cases. The process begins by asking people in the program, "Who knows a lot about _____? Who should I talk to?" By asking a number of people who else to talk with, the snowball gets bigger and bigger as you accumulate new information-rich cases. In most programs or systems, a few key names or incidents are mentioned repeatedly. Those people or events recommended as valuable by a number of different informants take on special importance. The chain of recommended informants will typically diverge initially as many possible sources are recommended, then converge as a few key names get mentioned over and over.

(7) Criterion sampling. The logic of criterion sampling is to review and study all cases that meet some predetermined criterion of importance. This approach is common in quality assurance efforts. For example, the expected range of participation in a mental health outpatient program might be 4 to 26 weeks. *All* cases that exceed 28 weeks are reviewed and studied to find out what is happening and to make sure the case is being appropriately handled.

Critical incidents can be a source of criterion sampling. For example, all incidents of client abuse in a program may be objects of in-depth evaluation in a quality assurance effort. All former mental health clients who commit suicide within three months of release may constitute a sample for in-depth, qualitative study. In a school setting, all students who are absent more than half the time may merit the in-depth attention of a qualitative case study.

The point of criterion sampling is to be sure to understand cases which are likely to be information rich because they may reveal major system weaknesses which become targets of opportunity for program or system improvement.

Criterion sampling can add an important qualitative component to a management information system or an ongoing program monitoring system. All cases in the data system that exhibit certain predetermined criterion characteristics are routinely identified for in-depth, qualitative analysis. Criterion sampling also can be applied to identify cases from quantitative questionnaires or tests for in-depth follow-up.

(8) Confirmatory and disconfirming cases. In the early part of qualitative fieldwork the evaluator is exploring—gathering data and beginning to allow patterns to emerge. Over time the exploratory state gives way to confirmatory fieldwork. This involves testing ideas, confirming the importance and meaning of possible patterns, and checking out the viability of emergent findings with new data and additional cases. This stage of fieldwork requires considerable rigor and integrity on the part of the evaluator in looking for and sampling confirmatory as well as disconfirming cases.

Confirmatory cases are additional examples which fit already emergent patterns; these cases confirm and elaborate the findings, adding richness, depth, and credibility. Disconfirming cases are no less important at this point. These are the examples which do not fit. They are a source of rival interpretations as well as a way of placing boundaries around confirmed findings. They may be "exceptions that prove the rule" or exceptions that disconfirm and alter what appeared to be important findings and viable interpretations prior to dealing with the case(s) that will not fit.

The source of questions or ideas to be confirmed or disconfirmed may originate with stakeholders rather than the evaluator's fieldwork. An evaluation may in part serve the purpose of confirming or disconfirming stakeholders' preconceptions, these having been identified early on in evaluator-stakeholder conceptual design discussions.

Thinking about the challenge of finding confirmatory and disconfirming cases emphasizes the relationship between sampling and evaluation conclusions. The sample determines what the evaluator will have something to say about, thus the importance of sampling carefully and thoughtfully.

(9) Sampling politically important cases. Evaluation is inherently and inevitably political to some extent (see Patton, 1986). A variation of the critical case strategy involves selecting (or sometimes avoiding) a politically sensitive site or unit of analysis. For example, a statewide program may have a local site in the district of a state legislator who is particularly influential. By studying carefully the program in that district, evaluation data may be more likely to attract attention and get used. This does not mean that the evaluator then undertakes to make that site look either good or bad, depending on the politics of the moment. This is simply an additional sampling strategy for trying to increase the usefulness and utilization of information where resources permit the study of only a limited number of cases.

(10) Convenience sampling. Finally, there is the strategy of sampling by convenience: doing what's fast and convenient. This is probably the most common sampling strategy—and the least desirable. Too often evaluators using qualitative methods think that since the sample size they can study is too small to permit generalizations it does not matter how cases are picked, so they might as well pick ones that are easy to access and inexpensive to study. While convenience and cost are real considerations, they should be the last factors to be taken into account after the evaluator and decision makers have carefully considered how they can strategically get the most information of greatest utility from the limited number of cases to be sampled. Purposeful, strategic sampling can yield crucial information about critical cases. Convenience sampling is neither purposeful nor strategic.

Information-Rich Cases

These are not the only ways of sampling qualitatively. The underlying principle that is common to all these strategies is selecting information-rich cases. These are cases from which one can learn a great deal about matters of importance in the evaluation.

Nor are these strategies mutually exclusive. Each approach serves a somewhat different purpose. Since evaluations often serve multiple purposes, more than one qualitative sampling strategy may be necessary. In long-term fieldwork all of these strategies may be used at some point.

The Credibility of Small, Purposeful Samples

The evaluator, in this process of developing the evaluation design, is trying to consider and anticipate the kinds of arguments that will lend credibility to the data and the kinds of arguments that will be used to attack the data. Reasons that are used to make site selections or individual case selections need to be carefully articulated and made explicit. Moreover, it is also important to make explicit the reasons why any particular sampling strategy may lead to distortions in the data— that is, to anticipate criticisms that will be made of a particular sampling strategy. Having weighed the evidence and considered the alternatives, evaluators and primary stakeholders make the sampling decision, sometimes painfully, but always with the recognition that there are no perfect designs.

There are no guidelines for determining the size of purposeful samples. This is a matter for negotiation with stakeholders, evaluation funders, decision makers, and information users. The sample should be large enough to be credible given the purpose of the evaluation, but small enough to permit adequate depth and detail for each case or unit in the sample. Variations in sample size will be discussed further in the chapters on interviewing and observation.

The fact that a small sample size must be chosen does not automatically mean that the sampling strategy should be purposeful instead of random. For many audiences random sampling, even of small samples, will substantially increase the credibility of the data. I recently worked with a program that annually appears before the state legislature and tells "war stories" about client successes, sometimes even including a few stories about failures to provide balance. The members of the program decided they wanted to begin collecting evaluation information. Because they are striving for individualized outcomes they rejected the notion of basing the evaluation entirely on some standardized pre-post instrument. They wanted to collect case histories and do in-depth case studies of clients, but they had very limited resources and time to devote to such data collection. In effect, staff at each program site, many of whom serve 200 to 300 families a year, felt that they could only do ten or fifteen detailed, in-depth clinical case histories each year. We systematized the kind of information that would be going into the case histories at each program site and then set up a random procedure for selecting those clients whose case histories would be recorded in depth. Essentially this program thereby systematized and randomized their collection of war stories. While they cannot generalize to the entire client population on the basis of ten cases from each program site, they will be able to tell legislators that the stories they are reporting were randomly selected in advance of knowledge of how the outcomes would appear, and the information collected was comprehensive. The credibility of systematic and randomly selected case examples is considerably greater than the personal, ad hoc selection of cases to report after the fact—that is, after outcomes are known.

Chapter 6, which discusses analysis, will deal with the problem of generalization as one analyzes and tries to make sense out of the data collected. It is too late, however, to make crucial design decisions about generalizations once one has begun analyzing the data. Decisions about what one wants to be able to say with the data, for what purpose, and with what degree of credibility are decisions that must be made in designing the evaluation.

Opportunistic Sampling

Fieldwork in evaluation often involves on-the-spot decisions about sampling to take advantage of new opportunities during actual data collection. Unlike experimental designs, qualitative methods and naturalistic inquiry designs can include new sampling strategies to take advantage of unforeseen opportunities after fieldwork has begun.

When doing observations it is not possible to capture everything. It is therefore necessary to make decisions about which activities to observe, which people to observe and interview, and what time periods will be selected to collect data. The strategies for making these decisions are actually the same as those used for sampling units of analysis. One can randomly sample time periods, activities, or people; or one can sample purposefully, deciding that certain activities are critical or certain key informants are more knowledgeable than others. Likewise, the observer may look for extreme cases, typical cases, or a variety of cases, activities, behaviors, or people. Indeed, once in the field, observers will frequently use all of these approaches at varying times for different parts of the data collection.

The importance of flexibility and creativity in considering sampling options leads directly to a consideration of more general design options and methodological mixes.

Design Alternatives and Methodological Mixes

There are strengths and weaknesses to any single data collection strategy. Using more than one data collection approach permits the evaluator to combine strengths and correct some of the deficiencies of any one source of data. Building checks and balances into a design through multiple data collection strategies is called *triangulation*. The triangle is the strongest of all geometric shapes, and triangulated evaluation designs are aimed at increasing the strength and rigor of an evaluation.

Triangulation

Denzin (1978a) has identified four basic types of triangulation: (1) *data triangulation*—the use of a variety of data sources in a study, for example, interviewing people in different status positions or with different points of view; (2) *investigator triangulation*—the use of several different evaluators or social scientists; (3) *theory triangulation*—the use of multiple perspectives to interpret a single set of data; and (4) *methodological triangulation*—the use of multiple methods to study a single problem or program, such as interviews, observations, questionnaires, and documents.

Denzin explains that the logic of triangulation is based on the premise that

no single method ever adequately solves the problem of rival causal factors. . . . Because each method reveals different aspects of empirical reality, multiple methods of observations must be employed. This is termed triangulation. I now offer as a final methodological rule the principle that multiple methods should be used in every investigation. (Denzin, 1978a, p. 28)

Triangulation is ideal. It is also very expensive. Most evaluation research involves quite limited budgets, short time frames, and political constraints. Certainly one important strategy for conducting evaluations is to employ multiple methods. But in the real world of limited resources, attempts at triangulation may mean a series of poorly implemented methods rather than one approach well executed. Where possible, triangulation is highly recommended. Indeed, the capability to implement a comprehensive strategy of triangulation means that evaluators must include in their repertoire of skills the ability to use qualitative methods.

**Variations on Qualitative Themes:
Pure Versus Mixed Strategies**

Triangulation is a powerful solution to the problem of relying too much on any single data source or method and thereby undermining the validity and credibility of findings because of the weaknesses of any single method. Triangulation is the recognition that the evaluator needs to be open to more than one way of looking at a program. A corollary to this insight is that purity of method is less important than dedication to relevant and useful information. Before presenting some of the ways in which a practical and utilitarian approach to evaluation may involve departures from methodological purity, it is worth considering the case for maintaining the integrity and purity of each methodological approach, model, or paradigm.

There are strong arguments for maintaining the integrity of a pure qualitative methods approach in evaluation. The themes of qualitative methods described in Chapter 1 do fit together into a cohesive approach. The openness and personal involvement of naturalistic inquiry mesh well with the openness and depth of qualitative data. Genuine openness flows naturally from an inductive approach to analysis, particularly an analysis grounded in the immediacy of direct fieldwork and sensitized to the desirability of holistic understanding of unique human settings. Likewise, there is an internal consistency and logic to quantitative-experimental designs which test deductive hypotheses built on theoretical premises. These premises identify the key variables to consider in measuring, controlling, and analyzing important program treatments and outcomes. The rules and procedures of the quantitative-experimental paradigm are aimed at producing internally valid, reliable, replicable, and generalizable findings.

Mixing parts of different approaches is a matter of some philosophical controversy. Yet, the practical mandate to gather the most relevant possible information to inform decision makers and stakeholders outweighs concerns about methodological purity based on epistemological and philosophical arguments. In practice it is altogether possible, and often desirable, to combine approaches. Let us first consider several ways in which variations on qualitative themes can be useful, then we shall consider ways in which qualitative and quantitative modes of inquiry can be combined.

Advocates of methodological purity argue that a single evaluator cannot be both deductive and inductive at the same time; one cannot be testing predetermined hypotheses and still remain open to whatever emerges from open-ended, phenomenological observation. Yet, in practice, human reasoning is sufficiently complex and flexible that it is possible to research predetermined questions and test hypotheses about certain aspects of a program while being quite open and naturalistic in pursuing other aspects of a program. In principle this is not greatly different from a questionnaire which includes both fixed alternative and open-ended questions. The extent to which a qualitative approach is inductive or deductive varies along a continuum. As evaluation fieldwork begins the evaluator may be open to whatever emerges from the data—a discovery or inductive approach. Then, as the inquiry reveals patterns and major dimensions of interest, the evaluator will begin to focus on verifying and elucidating what appears to be emerging—a more deductive approach to data collection and analysis.

The extent to which a study is "naturalistic" in design is also a matter of degree. This applies particularly with regard to the extent to which the evaluator places conceptual constraints on or makes presuppositions about the program. In practice, the naturalistic approach may often involve moving back and forth between inductive, open-ended, and phenomenological encounters with programs to more hypothetical-deductive attempts to verify "hypotheses" or solidify ideas which emerged from those more open-ended experiences, sometimes even manipulating something to see what happens. Thus naturalistic inquiry becomes a mixed strategy as the investigator moves back and forth between simply exploring and experiencing the program to engaging in data collection for purposes of verification and replication.

In the same vein, the attempt to understand specific cases or an entire program as a whole does not mean that the evaluator never becomes involved in component analysis or in looking at particular variables, dimensions, and parts of a program as separate entities. Rather, it means that the qualitative methodologist consciously works back and forth between parts and wholes, between separate variables and complex, interwoven constellations of variables in a sorting-out then putting-back-together process. Guided by the overarching strategy that mandates striving to present a holistic picture of the program, the qualitative evaluator recognizes that certain periods during data collection and analysis may focus on component, variable, and less-than-the-whole kinds of analysis.

The practice and practicalities of fieldwork also mean that the theme of "getting close" to the program under study is not an absolute and fixed approach. Closeness to and involvement with the people under study are most usefully viewed as variable dimensions. The personal styles and capabilities of evaluators will permit and necessitate variance along these dimensions. Variations in types of programs and evaluation purposes will affect the extent to which the evaluator can or should get close to people in the program. Moreover, closeness is likely to vary over the course of an evaluation. At times the evaluation fieldworker may become totally immersed in a program experience. These periods of immersion may be followed by times of withdrawal and distance (for personal as well as methodological reasons) to be followed still later by new experiences of immersion in and intimacy with the program being evaluated.

This spirit of adaptability and creativity in designing evaluations is aimed at being responsive to real-world conditions and meeting stakeholder information needs. It is in this spirit that we turn to some ways of combining elements of qualitative and quantitative methods.

Mixing Data Inquiry and Analysis Approaches

While triangulation is one way of increasing methodological power, a second approach is to borrow and combine parts from pure methodological strategies, thus creating mixed methodological approaches. To understand mixed methods it is helpful to separate the inquiry mode, data collection, and analysis components of the quantitative-experimental and qualitative-naturalistic approaches. The ideal-typical qualitative methods strategy consists of three parts: (1) qualitative data, (2) naturalistic inquiry, and (3) inductive content or case analysis. In contrast, the classic hypothetico-deductive approach to scientific inquiry would ideally include (1) quantitative data from (2) experimental (or quasi-experimental) research designs and (3) statistical analysis based on deductively derived hypotheses. (For a systematic comparison of the qualitative-naturalistic paradigm of research with the hypothetico-deductive paradigm see Patton, 1986.)

As already noted, there are strengths and virtues in the ideal or pure implementation of each approach. But there are also some important benefits to be gained by mixing methods and approaches. For example, suppose one wants to compare people who experience a certain innovation in a program with people who do not participate in the innovation, but the important variables on which to make the comparison are unclear. It is altogether possible—and even reasonable—to design an experiment with randomized assignment of subjects to treatment and control groups, yet to collect qualitative, open-ended data from those subjects. This means that experimental and quasi-experimental designs are entirely consonant with qualitative descriptions if the evaluator decides that the outcomes under study are best investigated by observing and recording the open-ended behavior and expressions of program participants.

Nor does the collection of descriptive and narrative data through in-depth interviewing and detailed observation presuppose a content analysis strategy of data analysis. It is possible to superimpose quantitative scales and dimensions onto qualitative data. Thus in the data analysis phase of a project the evaluator may decide to convert qualitative descriptions into quantitative scales that can be statistically manipulated. (See *How to Assess Program Implementation*, Volume 5 of the *Program Evaluation Kit*, for a description of this process.)

A variety of mixes, then, are possible—mixes of data type, inquiry mode, and analysis. Thus far these possible mixes have been described in relatively abstract terms. In order to make the choices available more clear, and in order to illustrate the creative possibilities that can emerge out of flexible approaches to research design, a number of brief examples of research strategies which involve mixes of data type, inquiry mode, and analysis are presented in the pages which follow. By no means are the examples provided meant to be exhaustive of the possibilities for constructing mixed methodological designs. Moreover, these examples have been constructed under the artificial constraint that *only one kind* of data type, inquiry mode, and analysis could be used in each case. In practice, of course, the possible mixes are much more varied because any given evaluation could include several types of data, variations in design, and mixed analytical approaches.

The Case of Operation Reach-Out:
An Example of Variations in Program Evaluation Design

With funds provided by United Way, local foundations, and the state government, a comprehensive program is established in a major city to serve high school age students who are educationally at high risk (poor grades, poor attendance, poor attitudes toward school); highly vulnerable in health terms (poor nutrition, sedentary life-style, high drug use); and likely candidates for problems with the criminal justice system (histories of juvenile delinquency, poor employment prospects, and alienation from dominant societal values).

The program consists of experiential educational internships through which these high risk students get individual attention, basic skills instruction, and part-time job placements which permit them to earn income while gaining work exposure. They also participate in peer group discussions aimed at changing health values, establishing a positive peer culture, and increasing social integration. The mandate for the program includes a requirement that the program be evaluated.

Six different evaluation design scenarios for this program are described below to illustrate different possible approaches.

(1) Pure Hypothetical-Deductive Approach to Evaluation:
Experimental Design, Quantitative Data,
and Statistical Analysis

The evaluator realizes that the program lacks sufficient resources to serve all needy youth in the target population. This provides an ethical justification for random admission into the program with those not admitted placed on a waiting list temporarily receiving no treatment intervention and therefore able to serve as a control group. Before the beginning of the program and again one year later, all youth, both those in the program and those in the control group, are administered standardized instruments measuring school achievement, self-esteem, anomie, alienation, and locus of control. Rates of school attendance, sickness, drug use, and delinquency are obtained for each group. When all data have been collected at the end of the year, comparisons between the control group and experimental group are made using inferential statistics with a level of .05 used as the criterion to determine statistically significant differences between the groups.

(2) Pure Qualitative Strategy:
Naturalistic Inquiry, Qualitative Data,
and Content Analysis

Procedures for recruiting and selecting participants into the program are determined entirely by the staff. The evaluator finds a convenient time to conduct an in-depth interview with participants as soon as they are admitted to the program. These in-depth interviews ask students to describe what school is like for them, what they do in school, how they typically spend their time, what their family life is like, how they approach academic tasks, their views about health, and their behaviors/attitudes with regard to delinquent and criminal activity. In brief, participants are asked to describe themselves and their social world. The evaluator finds out from program staff when the program activities will be taking place and observes the following: participant behaviors; participant conversations; staff behaviors; staff-participant interactions; and related phenomena. During the course of the program the evaluator finds informal opportunities for conducting additional in-depth interviews with participants to find out how they view the program, what kinds of experiences they are having, and what they are doing. Near the end of the program, in-depth interviews are conducted with the participants to find how they may have changed, how they view the world at this point in time, and what their expectations are for the future. In-depth interviews are also conducted with program staff. These data are content analyzed to find out what patterns of experience participants bring to the program, what patterns characterize their participation in the program, and what patterns of change are reported by and observed among the participants.

(3) Mixed Form:
Experimental Design, Qualitative Data Collection,
and Content Analysis

As in the pure experimental form (design 1), potential participants are randomly assigned to treatment and control groups. In-depth interviews are conducted with all youth—both those in the treatment group and those in the control group—before the program begins. The focus of those interviews is similar to that in the pure qualitative approach. Interviews are conducted again at the end of the program. Content analysis is performed separately on the data from the control group and the experimental group. The patterns found in the control group and the experimental group are then compared and contrasted.

(4) Mixed Form:
Experimental Design, Qualitative Data,
and Statistical Analysis

Participants are randomly assigned to treatment and control groups, and in-depth interviews are conducted both before the program and at the end of the program. These interview data in a raw form are then given to a panel of judges who rate each interview along several outcome dimensions operationalized as a ten-point scale. For both the preprogram interview and the postprogram interview, the panel of judges assign ratings on such dimensions as likelihood of success in school (low = 1, high = 10); likelihood of committing criminal offenses (low = 1, high = 10); commitment to education; commitment to engaging in productive work; self-esteem; and manifestation of desired nutritional and health habits. Inferential statistics are then used to compare these two groups. Judges made the ratings without knowledge of which participants were in the treatment group and which were in the control group. Outcomes on the rated scales are also statistically related to background characteristics of participants.

(5) Mixed Form:
Naturalistic Inquiry, Qualitative Data Collection,
and Statistical Analysis

As in the pure qualitative form, students are selected into the program on the basis of whatever criteria staff choose to apply. In-depth interviews are conducted with all students before the program and at the end of the program. These data are then submitted to a panel of judges who rate them on a series of dimensions such as those listed in the previous example. Change scores are computed for each individual and changes are statistically related to background characteristics of the students to determine in a regression format which characteristics of students are likely to predict success in the program. In addition, observations of program activities are rated on a set of scales developed to quantify the organizational attributes of activities—for example, the extent to which the activity involved active or passive participation; the extent to which student-teacher interaction was high or low; the extent to which interactions were formal or informal; and the extent to which participants had input into program activities. Ratings of activities based on qualitative descriptions are then aggregated to provide an overview of the treatment environment of the program.

(6) Mixed Form:
Naturalistic Inquiry, Quantitative Measurement, and Statistical Analysis

Students are selected into the program according to staff criteria. The evaluator enters the program setting without any predetermined categories of analysis or presuppositions about important variables or variable relationships. The evaluator observes important activities and events in the program, looking to see what types of behaviors and interactions will emerge. For each new type of behavior or interaction, the evaluator creates a category and then uses a time and space sampling design to count the frequency with which those categories of behavior and interaction are exhibited. The frequency of the manifestation of observed behaviors and interactions are then statistically related to such characteristics as group size, duration of the activity, staff-student ratios, and social/physical density.

Making Choices About Evaluation Design

The examples just listed provide only a few illustrations of possible design approaches. While it is possible to combine some methods, the same evaluation cannot employ an experimental design and naturalistic inquiry at the same time on the same program component and participants. Thus certain designs pose constraints that exclude other possibilities. It is not possible to create an experimental situation with random assignment to treatment and control groups yet at the same time to study the natural evolution of a setting.

The examples also illustrate another limitation on methodological combinations. It is possible to convert detailed, qualitative descriptions into quantitative scales for purposes of statistical analysis; it is not possible, however, to work the other way around and convert purely quantitative measures into detailed, qualitative descriptions.

Which evaluation design is best? Which strategy will provide the most useful answers? There is no simple, immediate, and universal answer to these questions. The answer in each case will depend on what stakeholders want to know, the purpose of the evaluation, the funds available, and the interests/abilities/biases of the evaluator(s) involved. What is certain is that different methods produce quite different information. The challenge is to find out which information is most needed and most useful in a given situation, and then to employ those methods best suited to producing the needed information.

For Further Reading

Cronbach, L. J. (1982). *Designing evaluations of educational and social programs.* San Francisco: Jossey-Bass.

Denzin, N. K. (1978). *The research act.* New York: McGraw-Hill.

Guba, E. G., & Lincoln, Y. S. (1981). *Effective evaluation: Improving the usefulness of evaluation results through responsive and naturalistic approaches.* San Francisco: Jossey-Bass.

Chapter 4
Fieldwork and Observation

Qualitative evaluations provide detailed descriptions of program activities, processes, and participants. An important source of qualitative evaluation data is direct, firsthand observation of the program. This means going "into the field," the "field" being wherever the program takes place. The evaluation observer takes careful and detailed field notes—the raw data of qualitative observation.

The quality of observational data is highly dependent on the skill, training, and competence of the evaluator. Fieldwork involves much more than the casual looking around we do in ordinary living. The trained observer is skilled in identifying and accurately describing meaningful human interactions and processes. In addition to training and practice the fieldworker needs concentration, patience, alertness, sensitivity and physical stamina. Observational fieldwork is hard work both physically and mentally. In discussions of the fallibility of human observation based on ordinary, nonscientific examples of observational deficiencies, the training, preparation, and intense effort of qualitative methods are often forgotten.

Observations by the Untrained and Unprepared

In a popular "guide for users of social science research" Katzer, Cook, and Crouch (1978) entitle their chapter on observation "Seeing Is Not Believing." In that chapter they tell an oft-repeated story that demonstrates what they consider to be the problem with observational data.

> Once at a scientific meeting, a man suddenly rushed into the midst of one of the sessions. He was being chased by another man with a revolver. They scuffled in plain view of the assembled researchers, a shot was fired, and they rushed out. About twenty seconds had elapsed. The chairperson of the session immediately asked all present to write down an account of what they had seen. The observers did not know that the ruckus had been planned,

rehearsed, and photographed. Of the forty reports turned in, only one was less than 20-percent mistaken about the principal facts, and most were more than 40-percent mistaken. The event surely drew the undivided attention of the observers, was in full view at close range, and lasted only twenty seconds. But the observers could not observe all that happened. Some readers chuckled because the observers were researchers but similar experiments have been reported numerous times. They are alike for all kinds of people. (Katzer et al., 1978, pp. 21-22)

This story is supposed to show that one cannot trust observational data: Human beings are unreliable observers. But what the story really demonstrates is that one cannot trust observations by the untrained and unprepared. What is often overlooked in stories such as this one about the inaccurate observations of researchers at a scientific meeting is that (1) these researchers were not *trained* as skilled observers and (2) they had not prepared themselves to make observations at that particular moment in time.

Scientific inquiry using observational methods requires disciplined training and rigorous preparation. The simple fact that a person is equipped with five functioning senses—sight, taste, hearing, smell, and touch—does not make that person a skilled observer. The fact that if several ordinary persons witness some event they will each report what they witnessed differently does not mean that *trained and prepared observers* cannot report with accuracy, validity, and reliability the nature of that event.

The Training and Preparation of a Skilled Observer

Training includes learning how to write descriptively, practicing the disciplined recording of field notes, knowing how to separate detail from trivia in order to achieve the former without being overwhelmed by the latter, and using rigorous methods to validate observations. Training researchers to become astute and skilled observers is particularly difficult because so many people think that they are "natural" observers and therefore have little to learn. Training to become a skilled observer is no less rigorous than training to become a skilled quantitative social scientist.

Careful preparation for making observations is as important as disciplined training. Preparation has intellectual, physical, psychological, and material dimensions. Noted scientist Louis Pasteur said, "In the fields of observation, chance favors the prepared mind." Part of preparing the mind is learning how to concentrate during the observation. A scientific observer cannot be expected to engage in scientific observation on the spur of the moment any more than a world class boxer can be expected to defend his title spontaneously on a street corner or an Olympic runner can be asked to dash off at record speed because someone suddenly thinks it would be nice to test the runner's time.

Two points, then, to keep in mind throughout this chapter. First, the popular wisdom about observation being nothing more than selective perception is true in the ordinary course of participating in day-to-day events. Second, the skilled observer is able to improve the accuracy, validity, and reliability of observations through disciplined training and rigorous preparation.

These distinctions are also important to make with stakeholders when discussing the strengths and weaknesses of various methods. The quality of *any* evaluation is highly dependent on the competence and professionalism of the evaluator. The quality of qualitative evaluations is particularly dependent on the training and preparation of the evaluation observer.

The Value of Observational Data

The purpose of observational evaluation data is first to *describe* the program thoroughly and carefully. This includes describing the activities that took place in the program, the people who participated in those activities, and the meaning to those people of what was observed. Observational evaluation reports must include sufficient descriptive detail to allow users of the report to know what has occurred and how it has occurred. The descriptions must be factual, accurate, and thorough without being cluttered by irrelevant minutia and trivia. The basic guideline to apply to a recorded observation is this: Write the description in a way that permits the reader to enter the observed situation.

The primary strength of naturalistic program observations is that the data are collected in the field, where the action is, as it happens. This is the characteristic that cuts across the various terms for gathering observational data:

> participant observation, field observation, qualitative observation, direct observation, or field research. All these terms refer to the circumstance of

being in or around an on-going social setting for the purpose of making a qualitative analysis of that setting. (Lofland, 1971, p. 93)

There are several advantages to observational fieldwork for evaluation purposes. First, by directly observing a program the evaluator is better able to understand the *context* within which program activities occur. Understanding context is essential to a holistic perspective.

Second, firsthand experience with a program allows the evaluator to be inductive in approach. This is the case because the observer, by being personally present, has less need to rely on prior conceptualizations of the setting. The observer can directly experience the program as an experience unto itself, thereby making the most of an inductive, discovery-oriented approach.

A third strength of observational methods is that the trained evaluator has the opportunity to see things that may routinely escape conscious awareness among participants in the program. In order for someone to report information in an interview they must be aware that they have the desired information. Because all social systems involve routines, participants in those routines may take them so much for granted that they cease to be aware of important nuances that are apparent only to an observer who has not been previously immersed in those routines.

A fourth value of direct observational approaches is the extent to which the observer can learn about things that program participants may be unwilling to talk about in an interview. The sensitivity of some topics in an interview may make interviewees unwilling or unable to provide important information. Through direct experience with and observation of actual events the evaluator can gain information that would otherwise not be available.

A fifth and closely related point is that observations permit the evaluator to move beyond the selective perceptions of others. Interviews present the understandings of the people being interviewed. Those understandings constitute important, indeed critical, information. However, it is necessary for the evaluator to keep in mind that interviewees are always reporting perceptions—often highly selective perceptions. Of course, evaluators as field observers may also have selective perceptions. By making their own perceptions part of the data, evaluators are able to present a more comprehensive view of the program being studied.

Finally, getting close to a social setting through firsthand experience permits the evaluator to access personal knowledge and direct experience as resources to aid in understanding and interpreting the program being observed. Reflection and introspection are important parts of field research. The impressions and feelings of the observer become part of the data to be used in attempting to understand a program and the people in it. The observer takes in information and forms impressions that go beyond what can be fully recorded in even the most detailed field notes. These understandings become important in analyzing the data and in making recommendations for program improvement. This latter point deserves emphasis. Recommendations based on qualitative data derived from firsthand program experience and observations ought to be especially valuable because they are grounded in direct understanding of program realities, not pie-in-the-sky, abstract ideals. Evaluation fieldwork should yield highly practical and relevant recommendations.

Variations in Observational Methods

Observational research is not a single thing. The decision to employ field methods in gathering information about a program is only the first step in a decision process that involves a large number of options and possibilities. Making the choice to employ field methods involves a commitment to get close to the program in its natural setting, to be factual and descriptive in reporting what is observed, and to find out the points of view of participants in the program observed. Once these fundamental commitments have been made, it is necessary to make additional decisions about which particular observational approaches are appropriate for the evaluation situation at hand.

**Variations in Observer Involvement:
Participant or Onlooker?**

The first and most fundamental distinction among observational strategies concerns the extent to which the evaluation observer is also a participant in the program activities being studied. This is not really a simple choice between participation and nonparticipation. The extent of participation is a continuum which varies from complete immersion in the program as full participant to complete separation from the activities observed, taking on a role as spectator; there is a great deal of variation along the continuum between these two extremes.

Nor is it simply a matter of deciding once and for all in a study how much the observer will participate. The extent of participation can change over time. In some cases the evaluator may begin as an onlooker and gradually become a participant as the study progresses. In other cases the evaluator may begin as a complete participant in order to experience what it is like to be initially immersed in the setting; as time passes the evaluator may gradually withdraw participation until finally assuming the role of occasional observer from a nonparticipant, onlooker stance.

Participant observation is an omnibus field strategy in that it "simultanteously combines document analysis, interviewing of respondents and informants, direct participation and observation, and introspection" (Denzin, 1978b, p. 183). In participant observation the evaluator shares as intimately as possible in the life and activities of the people in the program. The purpose of such participation is to develop an *insider's* view of what is happening. This means that the evaluator not only sees what is happening but *feels* what it is like to be part of the group.

Experiencing an environment as an insider is what necessitates the *participant* part of participant observation. At the same time, however, there is clearly an *observer* side to this process. The challenge is to combine participation and observation so as to become capable of understanding the experience as an insider while describing the experience for outsiders.

The extent to which it is possible for an evaluator to become a full participant in an experience will depend partly on the nature of the program being observed. For example, in human service and education programs that serve children, it is not possible for the evaluator to become a student and therefore experience the program as a child; it may be possible, however, for the evaluation observer to participate as a volunteer, parent, or staff person in such a program and thereby develop the perspective of an insider in one of these adult roles.

Programs that serve special populations may also involve natural limitations on the extent to which the evaluator can become a *full* participant. For example, an observer who is not chemically dependent will not be able to become a full participant in a chemical dependency program though it is possible for the participant-observer to actually experience the treatment and join the program as a client. Such participation in a treatment program can lead to important insights and understandings about what it is like to be in the program. Still, the evaluator must avoid the delusion that participation has been complete.

This point is illustrated by an exchange between a prisoner and a young evaluator who was doing participant observation in a prison.

Inmate: "What you here for, man?"

Evaluator: "I'm here for a while to find out what it's like to be in prison."

Inmate: "What you mean—'find out what it's like'?"

Evaluator: "I'm here so that I can experience prison from the inside instead of just studying what it's like from out there."

Inmate: "You got to be jerkin' me off, man. Experience from the inside? Shit, man, you can go home when you decide you've had enough can't you?"

Evaluator: "Yeah."

Inmate: "Then you ain't never gonna know what it's like from the inside."

There are also social and political factors which can limit participation. If the participants in a setting all know each other intimately they may object to an outsider trying to become part of their close circle. Where there are marked social class differences between the evaluator and program participants the people in the setting may object to the ruse of full participation. Program staff may object to the additional burden for them of having to include an evaluator in a program where resources are limited and staff-client ratios would be unbalanced by an additional participant.

The point here is that evaluators who adopt qualitative research strategies must avoid the fallacy of thinking that the *ideal* is always and only full and complete participation in the program, what is often called "going native." *The ideal is to negotiate and adopt that degree of participation which will yield the most meaningful data given the characteristics of the participants, the nature of questions to be studied, and the sociopolitical context of the setting.*

One final caution: The evaluator's plans and intentions regarding the degree of program involvement to be experienced may not be the way things actually turn out. Lang and Lang (1960) reported that two scientific participant-observers who were studying audience behavior at a Billy Graham evangelical crusade made *their* "decision for Christ" and left their observer posts to walk down the aisle and join the Reverend Graham's campaign. Such are the occupational hazards (or benefits, depending on your perspective) of observation research.

Overt and Covert Observations

A major concern about the validity and reliability of observational data concerns the effects of the observer on what is observed. The basic notion here is that people may behave quite differently when they know they are being observed compared to how they behave if they are not aware of being observed. Thus, the argument goes, covert observations are more likely to capture what is really happening than are overt observations which allow people in the program to become aware that they are being studied.

There are a full range of opinions concerning the ethics and morality of conducting covert research. On one end of the continuum is the absolute opposition by Edward Shils to all forms of covert research. He opposes any "observations of private behavior, however technically feasible, without the explicit and fully informed permission of the person to be observed"; he argues that there should be full disclosure of the purpose of any research project and argues that even the technique of participant observation is "morally obnoxious . . . manipulation" unless the observer makes explicit his research questions at the very beginning of the observation (Shils, 1959; quoted in Webb, 1966, p. vi).

At the other end of the continuum is the "investigative social research" approach of Jack Douglas (1976). Douglas argues that conventional anthropological field methods have been based upon a consensus view of society which assumes that people are basically cooperative and helpful, willing to have their points of view understood and shared with the rest of the world. In contrast to the consensus model Douglas adopts a conflict paradigm of society which leads him to believe that any and all covert methods of research should be considered acceptable options in a search for truth.

> The investigative paradigm is based on the assumption that profound conflicts of interest, values, feelings, and actions pervade social life. It is taken for granted that many of the people one deals with, perhaps all people to some extent, have good reason to hide from others what they are doing and even to lie to them. Instead of trusting people and expecting trust in return, one suspects others and expects others to suspect him. Conflict is the reality of life; suspicion is the guiding principle. . . . It's a war of all against all and no one gives anyone anything for nothing, especially truth. (Douglas, 1976, p. 55)

Explicitness About Research Purpose

Just as participation is not an either-or choice in observational research, so the degree of explicitness about observations and the purpose of an evaluation is not an either-or proposition. The extent to which participants in a program are informed that they are being observed and told the purpose of the evaluation ranges from full disclosure to no disclosure, with a great deal of variation along the middle of this continuum.

The complexities of evaluation research mean that there are several levels at which decisions about the covert-overt nature of observations and the explicit versus hidden purpose of the evaluation can be made. Sometimes only the funders of the evaluation know the full extent and purpose of observations. On other occasions key people in the program may be informed that an observer will be participating, but others will not be so informed. In still other cases an evaluator may reveal the purpose and nature of participation to low status participants and ask for their cooperation in keeping the study secret from high status or other powerful persons. Sometimes the situation becomes so complex that the evaluator may lose track of who knows and who does not know; and, of course, there are the classic comedy situations where everyone involved knows that a study is being done and who the observer is—but the observer does not know that everyone else knows!

Finally, there is the related issue of confidentiality. Those who advocate covert research or keeping secret the purpose of the evaluation usually do so with the condition that reports conceal names, locations, and other identifying information so that the people who have been observed will be protected from harm or punitive action. In evaluation research, however, while the identity of who said what may be possible to keep secret, it is more difficult, and indeed may defeat the purpose of the evaluation.

Evaluators have to resolve these issues in each case in accordance with their own consciences, evaluation purposes, political realities, and ethical sensitivities. In so doing, it is important to keep in mind the ethical standards for the conduct of evaluations developed by the Joint Committee on Standards for Educational Evaluation:

- Evaluations should be designed and conducted so that the rights and welfare of the human subjects are respected and protected. (Joint Committee, 1981, p. 81)
- Evaluators should respect human dignity and worth in their interactions with other persons associated with an evaluation. (Joint Committee, 1981, p. 86)
- Evaluation findings should be disseminated to clients and other right-to-know audiences, so that they can assess and use the findings. (Joint Committee, 1981, p. 20)

Variations in Duration of Observations

Another important dimension along which observational studies vary is the length of time devoted to data-gathering. In the anthropological tradition of field research a participant-observer expects to spend a minimum of six months and often years living in the culture being observed. In sociological studies of subcultures studies vary in length from months to years. To develop a holistic view of an entire culture or subculture takes a great deal of time. The purpose of basic research in the social sciences using field methods is to unveil the basic complexities and patterns of social reality. The social scientist engaged in the conduct of basic research hopes to generate and verify theoretical propositions about how cultures and societies function.

At the other end of the continuum is program evaluation. The purpose of program evaluation is usually more modest: generating useful information for action. To be useful, evaluation information must be timely. Decision makers cannot wait for years while fieldworkers sift through mountains of field notes. Many evaluations are conducted under enormous pressures of time and limited resources. Where observational data have been selected as the appropriate kind of information for a particular evaluation problem the duration of the observations will depend to a considerable extent on the time and resources available in relation to the information needs of primary stakeholders. While some evaluation projects may involve years of study accumulating detailed data throughout the life of a program, other studies may involve observations of a single one- or two-hour segment of a program. Evaluations that include brief site visits to a number of program locations may serve the purpose of simply establishing the existence of various levels of program operations at different sites.

The critical point about the duration of observational studies is that the length of time during which observations take place should follow from the nature of the evaluation questions being studied and not from some idea about what a typical participant observation must necessarily involve. At times and for certain programs long-term fieldwork is essential. At other times and for other programs it may be helpful for program staff to have a highly skilled and perceptive formative evaluator provide feedback based on as little as one hour of onlooker observation. Clearly the depth, detail, and sensitivity of data will vary accordingly.

Variations in Observational Focus

The preceding sections have discussed how observations vary in four ways: the extent to which the observer participates in the program being evaluated; the extent to which fieldwork is overt or covert; the extent to which the purpose of the evaluation is made explicit; and the duration of the observations. A major factor affecting each of these other dimensions is the scope or focus of the study. As noted in the design chapter, the scope of an evaluation can be quite broad, encompassing virtually all aspects of the program, or it can be quite narrow, involving a look at only some small part of what is going on in a program.

The tradition of anthropological field studies emphasizes the importance of trying to capture the holistic essence of a culture. The various subsystems of a society are thus understood as interdependent parts such that the economic subsystem, the belief subsystem, the political subsystem, the kinship subsystem, and other specialized subsystems are best described and interpreted in relation to each other. In practice, however, fieldwork observations typically tend to focus on a particular part of the society or culture depending on investigator interests and the practicalities of allocating time differentially to those things which the researcher considers most important. Thus a particular study might present an overview of a particular culture but then go on to report in greatest detail on the religious system of that culture.

Likewise, decisions about the focus and scope of an evaluation necessarily vary from very broad to very narrow. The problem is to determine the extent to which it is desirable and useful to study one or a few questions in great depth or to study many questions but with less depth. The next major section on "What to Observe" discusses in detail some of the alternatives possible in focusing observations. The extent to which the focus of observations is broad or narrow depends on the resources available, time available, and the purpose of the evaluation. The evaluation focus will then determine to a great extent which of the many fieldwork design options is both practical and useful.

Dimensions Along Which Fieldwork Varies: Summary

Five primary dimensions can be used to describe major variations in fieldwork observations. Those dimensions, discussed in the previous sections, are graphically summarized in Figure 4.1. These five dimensions can be used to help make decisions about the parameters of a particular evaluation. They can also be used to review how the

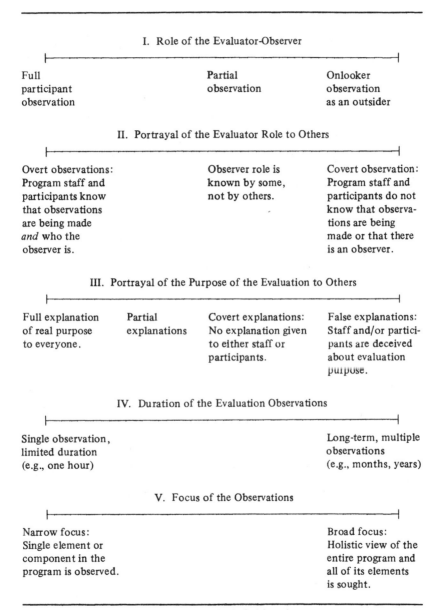

I. Role of the Evaluator-Observer

| Full participant observation | Partial observation | Onlooker observation as an outsider |

II. Portrayal of the Evaluator Role to Others

Overt observations: Program staff and participants know that observations are being made *and* who the observer is.

Observer role is known by some, not by others.

Covert observation: Program staff and participants do not know that observations are being made or that there is an observer.

III. Portrayal of the Purpose of the Evaluation to Others

Full explanation of real purpose to everyone.

Partial explanations

Covert explanations: No explanation given to either staff or participants.

False explanations: Staff and/or participants are deceived about evaluation purpose.

IV. Duration of the Evaluation Observations

Single observation, limited duration (e.g., one hour)

Long-term, multiple observations (e.g., months, years)

V. Focus of the Observations

Narrow focus: Single element or component in the program is observed.

Broad focus: Holistic view of the entire program and all of its elements is sought.

Figure 4.1 Five dimensions along which fieldwork varies.

evaluation is proceeding along each dimension during the course of the study and following the completion of observations.

What to Observe

It is not possible to observe everything. The human observer is not a movie camera, and even a movie camera has to be pointed in the right direction to capture what is happening. Moreover, a movie camera has a limited field of vision, taking in only those activities that can be seen within that field accessible to it. For both the human observer and the camera there must be focus. In evaluation this focus is provided in part by the evaluation questions being asked. Before entering the field, the evaluator must somehow organize the complex reality represented by the program so that the observations are both manageable and relevant to the purpose of the evaluation.

The purpose of this section is to identify some areas within which observations can be focused. These options about what to observe are cues that can help sensitize the observer to information that may be needed to adequately describe a program and its participants.

Experienced observers learn that certain kinds of activities and events are likely to yield particularly useful information and insights. When a strategy for placing particular emphasis on certain kinds of observations is made explicit it often involves what qualitative methodologists call "sensitizing concepts." Rather than being preordinate categories or operationalized variables, sensitizing concepts provide a basic framework highlighting the importance of certain kinds of events, activities, and behaviors. Group process is a sensitizing concept. Kinship, leadership, socialization experiences, power, and similar notions are sensitizing in that they alert us to ways of organizing the experience and making decisions about what to record. The sections which follow present sensitizing categories for evaluation fieldwork.

Describing the Program Setting

The description of the setting observed should be sufficiently detailed to permit the reader to visualize that setting. The inclusion of quotations from participants about their reactions to and perceptions of that environment may be particularly useful. Photographs are also helpful if taken unobtrusively.

A good exercise for beginning observers is to write a description of some setting and share it with other people, asking them if they can visualize the setting described. Likewise, it is helpful to have two people observe the same environment and share descriptions, watching in particular for the use of interpretive or abstract adjectives (e.g., a "positive" environment) instead of descriptive ones (e.g., a downtown storefront office). Learning to be descriptive means providing sufficient information that the reader does not have to guess at what the observer means or supply a great deal of additional information to interpret the description. For example, "a crowded room" is an interpretive evaluation statement. The description should have reported this:

> The room was large enough for a three-person couch across one side, six chairs on the walls next to the couch, and three chairs by the wall facing the couch, which included the door. With twenty people in the room, each person had space to fit, but when everyone was standing there was very little space between people. Several participants were overheard to say, "this room is too crowded."

The physical environment of a social setting can be quite important to what happens in that environment. A common mistake among evaluation observers is to take the physical environment for granted. Thus a researcher may report that the program took place in "a school." The observer may have a mental image of "school" that matches what was observed, but schools vary considerably in size, appearance, and neighborhood setting. Even more so, the interiors of schools vary considerably. The same can be said for criminal justice settings, health settings, community mental health programs, and any other social setting.

The Human, Social Environment

Just as physical environments vary, so too do the social environments of programs. The ways in which human beings interact create social ecological constellations that affect how participants behave toward each other in those environments. In describing the social environment the observer looks for the ways in which people organize themselves into groups and subgroups. Patterns of interaction, frequency of interactions, the direction of communication patterns, and changes in these patterns reveal things about the social environment. The characteristics of people in these different groupings, male-female interactions, interactions among people with different background characteristics, different racial characteristics, and of different ages alert the observer to patterns in the social ecology of the program.

Decision-making patterns can be a focus of particular interest in a social environment. Who makes decisions about the activities that take place? How are decisions communicated?

As with the physical environment it is important that the observer maintain a distinction between a description of what has happened in the setting and reporting on the perceptions of participants about what has happened. The observer's descriptions of a setting's social environment will not necessarily be the same as the perceptions of that environment expressed by participants. Indeed, it is unlikely that all participants will perceive the social environment in the same way. At all times it is critical that the observer record participant perceptions in quotation marks, indicating the source of those perceptions, so as to keep such observations separate from the observer's own descriptions and interpretations of the situation.

Program Activities and Participant Behaviors

The central focus in most program observations is on program activities and participant behaviors. What do people in the program do? What are their experiences? What is it like to be a participant in the setting observed? What activities take place? These are the kinds of questions evaluators bring to the program setting as they begin to observe program implementation.

In describing program activities it is usually necessary to find units of activity that have a kind of unity about them. Activities involve some chronological sequence of events; they typically have a beginning, some middle point, and a closure point. In observing a program the evaluator looks for these units of activity. They will usually have specially designated labels given to them either by staff or participants, but sometimes the evaluator will discover units of activity embedded within larger events. Units of activity may be, for example, a class session, a counseling session, meal time in a residential facility, a meeting of some kind, a home visit in an outreach program, a consultation, or a registration procedure. In brief, these are the formal activities of the program.

In observing interactions and activities the evaluator attempts to capture a comprehensive overview of what takes place in the observed activity. In order for the descriptions of interactions to be comprehensive, information about the full sequence of events must be included: How is the activity introduced or the interaction begun? Who is present at the beginning? What exactly was said at the beginning? How did participants respond or react to what was said? These are the questions that focus the beginning of an activity.

These same kinds of questions stay before the observer throughout the full sequence of an observation. Who is involved? What is said? What happens? What do participants do? What are the variations in how participants are engaged in this activity? (The participant-observer records his or her own feelings as part of the data of observation.) How did behaviors and interactions change over the course of the activity?

Finally, the observer looks for closure points. What are the signals that the activity or interaction is being ended? Who is present at that time? What is said? How do participants react to the ending of the activity? How is the completion of this unit of activity related to other program activities and interactions?

It is helpful to treat units of activity as self-contained events for the purpose of observation. The process of looking for patterns across units of activity is the process of analysis. During the initial stages of an observation the evaluator will be kept busy just trying to capture self-contained units of activity without looking for the patterns and relationships among those activities that will emerge later from the analysis.

This section has been concerned with observing formal program activities that have marked beginnings and recognizable points of closure. Such formal activities constitute the main programmatic content of human service programs. The implementation of a program typically consists of a series of formal, planned activities. To understand a program and its effects on participants, however, the evaluation observer cannot be restricted to formal, planned activities. The next section discusses the observation of the things that go on between and around formal, planned program activities.

Informal Interactions and Unplanned Activities

If evaluation observers put away their seeing and observing selves as soon as a program activity ends, they will miss a great deal of data. Some programs build in "free time," or unstructured time, between activities to allow participants to assimilate what has occurred during formal programmatic activities and to provide participants (and staff) with necessary breathing room. Other programs do not recognize the programmatic potential for unstructured time, but it is the rare program or institution that can plan every moment of participants' time.

During periods of informal interaction and unplanned activity it can be particularly difficult to organize observations because people are likely to be milling around, coming and going, moving in and out of small groups, with some sitting alone, some writing, some seeking refreshments, and all variously engaging in a full range of what may appear to be random behaviors. How, then, can the evaluator-observer collect data during such a time?

This situation illustrates beautifully the importance of staying open to the data. It is impossible to anticipate what kinds of things might emerge during observation of unplanned activity time. Without attempting to interpret in advance or attach significance to participant behaviors at a moment in time, the observer simply continues to gather descriptive information about what people do and, in particular, what people are saying to each other.

This last point is especially important. It is during periods of unplanned program time that participants have the greatest opportunity to exchange views and to talk with each other about what they are experiencing in the program. In some cases the evaluator will simply listen in on the conversation of others. In some cases it may be appropriate to conduct informal interviews, either with a single participant in natural conversation or with some small group of people. At such times the evaluator asks normal, conversational questions: "So what did you think of what went on this morning?" "Was it clear to you what they were trying to get at?" "What did you think of the session today?" "How do you think what went on today fits into this whole thing that we're involved in?"

At the same time it is important to remember that everything that goes on in and around the program is data. The meaning, pattern, and significance of the data will vary, but there is still activity there, human experience, and program dynamics. The fact that none of the participants talk about a session when it is over is data. The fact that people immediately split in different directions when a session is over is data. The fact that people talk about personal interests and share gossip that has nothing to do with the program is data.

It is also not at all unusual in many kinds of programs for the most significant participant learning to go on during unstructured program time. A personal interaction with another participant may be the most important event that occurs during a program. To capture a holistic view of the program the evaluator-observer must stay alert to these periods of informal, unplanned activity.

Participant observation is necessarily a combination of observing and informal interviewing. It is important that evaluator-observers do not make assumptions about the meaning of what they observe without including directly from participants their perspectives about their own behaviors and experiences.

The Language of Program Participants

It is an axiom of anthropology that one cannot understand another culture without understanding the language of the people in that culture. Language is a way of organizing the world. The things for which people have words tell people what is important to that culture and that group. Thus the Eskimos have many words for snow and Arabs have many words for camel. Likewise, the artist has many words for red and many words to describe different kinds of brushes. Evaluators have many words for different kinds of evaluations.

The same phenomenon is observable in human service and education programs. Different program areas have their own language to describe the problems they deal with in their work. People who work with the mentally retarded have a complex system of language to distinguish different types of retardation. People in the criminal justice area have their own language for differentiating different types of offenders and different kinds of treatment. Part of the task of observation in a program is learning the native language of the program. This means learning not only the literal meanings of the words used but also the connotations and symbolism involved in those words for people in the program. It is not at all unusual in a program for participants to create their own words to describe particular aspects of their experience or of the program. The field notes of the observer should include the exact language used by participants to describe their experiences so that patterns of word usage can emerge in the analysis and so that the reader of the evaluator's observations can be given the flavor of native program language.

Using the precise language of participants is an important way to record participants' own understandings of their experiences. Observers must learn the language of participants in the program they are observing and record that language and its patterns in order to represent participants in their own terms and be true to the world view of participants.

Nonverbal Communication

Social and behavioral scientists have reported at length on the importance of both verbal and nonverbal kinds of communications in human groups. While recording the language of participants it is important that the evaluator also observe nonverbal forms of communication. In educational settings, for example, nonverbal communications would include patterns that are established for students to get the attention of or otherwise approach instructors. In group settings a great deal of fidgeting, moving about, and trying to get comfortable can communicate things about attention to and concentration on the group process. The way in which participants dress, express affection, physically space themselves in discussions, and arrange themselves in their physical setting are nonverbal cues.

The evaluator's own feelings about and reactions to nonverbal cues are an important part of the data in observations. The observer should record his or her own reactions to others. Also, combining observing with interviewing, it is often appropriate to ask people about their nonverbal behaviors and reactions to the nonverbal behaviors of others. By watching for patterns of behavior and *describing* what people are doing in different situations, the observer will be able to isolate those nonverbal behaviors that have special significance in a particular program setting.

Unobtrusive Measures

Program evaluation creates considerable anxiety among many program staff and participants. Regardless of how sensitively the evaluation is conducted, there is always the possibility that people will behave differently under conditions where an evaluation is taking place than they would if no evaluation were taking place. In their well-known book *Unobtrusive Measures: Non-Reactive Research in the Social Sciences,* (1966) Webb et al. suggest,

> Even when he is well-intentioned and cooperative, the research subject's knowledge that he is participating in a scholarly search may confound the investigator's data. . . . It is important to note early that the awareness of testing need not, by itself, contaminate responses. It is a question of probabilities, but the probability of bias is high in any study in which a respondent is aware of his subject status. (1966, p. 13)

It is concern about participants' reactions to observations that leads some social scientists to recommend covert research (as discussed earlier in this chapter). If participants are not aware that data collection is taking place, and are not aware that they are being observed, then reactivity is less of a threat to the validity of the evaluation. Even when participants are aware, however, that observations are taking place, there are often opportunities to make unobtrusive measurements. Unobtrusive measures are those that are made without the knowledge of the people being observed.

Robert L. Wolf and Barbara Tymitz (1977), for example, included unobtrusive measures in their natural inquiry study of the National Museum of Natural History at the Smithsonian Institute. They looked for "wear spots" as indicators of use of particular exhibit areas. They decided that worn rugs would indicate the popularity of particular areas in the museum.

The creative evaluator can learn a number of things about a setting by looking for physical clues about activities. Dusty equipment or records may indicate things that are not used. Areas that are used a great deal by children in a school will look different, more worn, than areas that are little used. The physical layout of a program will provide clues to important interaction patterns and may indicate significant status differences. For example, office furniture differences, the comparative location of offices, and special amenities can reveal important relationship and status arrangements

The search for unobtrusive measures illustrates that fieldwork is not a routine activity. The creative evaluator, aware of the variety of things one can learn from studying physical and social settings, may learn a great deal through attention to unobtrusive indicators of human activity.

Program Documents

It has already been noted that observation in the field includes looking and listening, observing and interviewing. The purpose of fieldwork is to find out as much as possible about what is happening in the program. In many cases program records and documents are another particularly rich source of information. The nature of program records and documents will vary from program to program, but in contemporary society all programs leave a trail of paper that the evaluator can follow and use to increase knowledge and understanding about the program.

It is important at the very beginning of the evaluation to negotiate access to program documents and records. The evaluator should attempt to anticipate as many different sources of information as possible. The ideal situation would include access to all routine records on clients, all correspondence from and to program staff, financial records, organizational rules, regulations, memoranda, charts, and any other official or unofficial documents generated by or for the program. These kinds of program documents provide the evaluator with information about many things that cannot be observed because they may have taken place before the evaluation began; because they include private interchanges to which the evaluator is not directly privy; and because they reflect aspects of the organization that may be idealized in formal documents but are not being realized in actual program performance and thus might be unknown to the evaluator.

Program documents provide valuable information because of what the evaluator can learn directly by reading them; but they also provide stimulus for generating questions that can only be pursued through direct observations and interviewing. Thus program records and documents serve a dual purpose: (1) they are a basic source of information about program activities and processes, and (2) they can give the evaluator ideas about important questions to pursue through more direct observations and interviewing.

As with all information to which an evaluator has access during observations, the confidentiality of program records—particularly client records—must be respected. The extent to which an evaluator will include actual references to and quotations from program records and documents in a final report needs to be negotiated on the basis of which documents ought to be considered part of the public record of the program being studied and therefore able to be publicized without breach of confidentiality. The paper traces that are the spoor of contemporary organizations are part of the information resources available to the field evaluator. Learning how to use, study, and understand these traces is part of the repertoire of skills needed by the evaluator who does fieldwork.

Observing What Does Not Happen

The preceding sections have been concerned with the things that one can observe. Observing what happens in a group, variations in activities, what people say, what they do, how they interact, and the nature of the physical setting are all important in a comprehensive approach to fieldwork. It is also often important to observe *what does not happen.*

This can be tricky. Once one ventures into the area of observing what does not happen, there are a near-infinite number of things one could point out in the area of "absence of occurrence."

There are two conditions under which it is appropriate and helpful to point out what has not occurred in a program. First, if the evaluator has prior knowledge suggesting that certain things ought to happen or are expected to happen, then it is appropriate to note that those things did not happen. If a school program is, according to its funding mandate, supposed to provide children with opportunities to explore the community, and no such explorations of the community occur, then it is appropriate for the observer to note that no such community activities occurred. If the evaluator reported only what occurred, a question might be left in the mind of the reader about whether or not the other activities had occurred but had not been observed. Likewise, if a criminal justice program is supposed to provide one-to-one counseling to juveniles, and no such counseling takes place, it is entirely appropriate for the evaluator to note the absence of this counseling.

The second condition under which it is appropriate to note that something did *not* occur is when the evaluator's basic experience and common sense suggest to him or her that the absence of some particular activity or factor is noteworthy. For example, if over time the observer notes ongoing harmony and consensus among a group of people, it is worth making clear in the observations that "no conflicts or personality hassles were observed in the interactions among group members." The reason for reporting this observation about what did not occur is to make it clear to the reader that the data have not been selected only to reflect interactions of consensus and harmony. The absence of interpersonal conflict among people in groups where there is considerable potential for conflict is worth reporting.

In many such cases the observation about what did not occur is simply a restatement, in the opposite, of what did occur. That restatement, however, will attract attention in a way that the initial observation might not. For example, if one were observing a program being conducted in a multiracial community, it is possible that program goals would include sensitivity on the part of staff to the needs, interests, and cultural differences of minorities, but there may not be specific mention about the desired racial composition of program staff. If, then, the evaluator observes that the staff of the program consists entirely of Caucasians, it is appropriate to make two kinds of observations: It is appropriate (1) to describe the staff as "Caucasian" and (2) to point out that "there were no representatives of minorities on the program staff." The second observation states something about what did not occur.

Likewise, if program planning processes never include participants' input in any systematic or direct way, it may well be appropriate for the evaluator to point out the absence of such input based on experience indicating the significance of participant input in the planning processes of other programs.

Doing Fieldwork:
The Data-Gathering Process

Field Notes

There are many options in the mechanics of taking field notes: the kind of writing materials used; the time and place at which field notes are taken; the symbols developed by the observer as his or her own method of shorthand; and how field notes are stored. It is impossible to provide universal prescriptions about the mechanics of and procedures for taking field notes because different settings lend themselves to different ways of proceeding and because the precise organization of fieldwork is very much a matter of personal style and individual work habits. *What is not optional is the taking of field notes!*

> Aside from getting along in the setting, the fundamental concrete task of the observer is the taking of field notes. Whether or not he performs this task is perhaps the most important determinant of later bringing off a qualitative analysis. Field notes provide the observer's *raison d'être*. If he is not doing them, he might as well not be in the setting. (Lofland, 1971, p. 102)

Field notes are the description of what has been observed. The field notes should contain everything that the observer believes to be worth noting. Do not trust anything to future recall. At the moment one is writing it is very tempting, because the situation is still fresh, to believe that the details or particular elements of the situation can be recalled later. If it is an important part of your consciousness as an observer—if it is information that has helped you understand the context, the program, what went on, whatever—then as soon as possible, that information should be put into the field notes.

First and foremost, field notes are descriptive. They should be dated and record such basic information as where the observation took place, who was present, what the physical setting was like, what social interactions occurred, what activities took place, and other descriptive information that will permit the observer to return mentally to that setting later through the field notes. The result is that field notes eventually permit the reader of the evaluation findings to experience the activity observed through edited and organized field notes in the evaluation report.

The following passages illustrate different kinds of descriptive field notes. On the left side are vague and overgeneralized field notes; on the right side are field notes, from the same observation, that are detailed and concrete.

Vague and Overgeneralized Notes

(1) The new client was uneasy waiting for her intake interview.

Detailed and Concrete Notes

(1) At first the client sat very stiffly on the chair next to the receptionist's desk. She picked up a magazine and let the pages flutter through her fingers very quickly without really looking at any of the pages. She set the magazine down, looked at her watch, pulled her skirt down, and picked up the magazine again. This time she didn't look at the magazine. She set it back down, took out a cigarette and began smoking. She would watch the receptionist out of the corner of her eye, and then look down at the magazine, and back up at the two or three other people waiting in the room. Her eyes moved from people to the magazine to the cigarette to the people to the magazine in rapid succession. She avoided eye contact. When her name was finally called she jumped like she was startled.

(2) The client was quite hostile toward the staff person.

(2) When the staff member told her that she could not do what she wanted to do, the client began to yell at the staff member, telling her that she couldn't control her life, that she was nothing but on a "power trip," that she'd "like to beat the shit out of her," and that

	she could just "go to hell." She shook her fist in her face and stomped out of the room, leaving the staff person standing there with her mouth open, looking amazed.
(3) The next student who came in to take the test was very poorly dressed.	(3) The next student who came into the room was wearing clothes quite different from the three students who'd been in previously. The three previous students looked like they came dressed for a professional experience. Their hair was combed, their clothes were clean and pressed, the colors of their clothes matched, their clothes were in good repair. This new student had on pants that were soiled, with a hole or tear in one knee and threadbare seat. The flannel shirt was wrinkled, with one tail tucked into the pants and the other tail hanging out. Hair was disheveled and the boy's hands looked like he'd been playing in the engine of a car.

These examples illustrate the problem of using general terms to describe specific actions and conditions. Words like "poor," "anger," and "uneasy" are not descriptive. Such interpretive words conceal what actually went on rather than reveal the details of the situation. Such terms have very little meaning for the person who is not present. Moreover, the use of such terms in field notes without the accompanying detailed description means that the fieldworker is recording primarily interpretations rather than description. Particularly revealing are terms that can only make sense in comparison to something else. To describe someone as "poorly" dressed it is necessary to have a frame of reference about what constitutes "good" dress. No skill is more critical in fieldwork than learning to be descriptive, concrete, and detailed. First and foremost, then, field notes are descriptive.

Second, field notes contain what people said. Direct quotations, or as near as possible recall of direct quotations, should be included in the field notes. These quotations will come from what people said during activities as well as what they said during interviews, both informal and formal.

Third, field notes contain the evaluator's own feelings, reactions to the experience, and reflections about the meaning and significance of what has occurred. Again, it is critical that you not deceive yourself that you can conjure up those feelings again simply by reading the descriptions of what took place. Record your feelings and reactions at the time you experience them, while you are in the field. Record their nature and their intensity. In naturalistic inquiry the observer's own experience is a crucial part of the data. Part of the purpose of getting close to the program and close to the participants in the program through fieldwork is to permit the evaluator to experience what it is like to be in the program. If what the experience is like for the observer is not recorded in the field notes, then an important purpose for being there is lost.

Finally, field notes include the observer's insights, interpretations, beginning analyses, and working hypotheses about what is happening in the program. The observer's primary responsibilities are to experience and describe what is going on in the program. The observer approaches fieldwork with a disciplined intention not to impose preconceptions or make premature judgments. Nevertheless, the observer does not simply booome a recording machine upon entering the field. Insights, ideas, inspirations, and—yes, judgments, too!—will occur while making notes.

Observers need to schedule the writing of field notes without unduly affecting either their participation or the quality of their observations. Given these constraints, the basic rule of thumb is to write promptly, to complete field notes as soon and as often as is physically and programmatically possible. Writing field notes is rigorous and demanding work that requires personal discipline and time—as much or more time than that taken by the observations!

Using Key Informants

At any stage of fieldwork key informants can be an important source of information. Key informants are people who are particularly knowledgeable and articulate, people whose insights can prove particularly useful in helping an observer understand what is happening. One of the mainstays of fieldwork is the use of key informants as sources of information about what the evaluation observer has not or cannot experience, as well as a source of explanation for things that the observer has actually witnessed.

The selection of key informants must be done carefully so as to avoid arousing political hostility or personal antagonisms among others. It is not necessary to announce formally that the "position" of key informant has been filled. The key informant is simply that person or those persons with whom the observer is likely to spend some considerable time talking about what is happening in the program. Key informants must often be trained in their role.

Key informants can be a particularly useful way of finding out what is happening in subgroups to which the observer does not or cannot have direct access. The danger in using key informants is that their perspectives will be distorted and biased, thus giving an inaccurate picture of what is happening. It is important that information obtained from key informants be clearly specified as such in the observer's fieldwork notes ("The informant said that . . ."). Data obtained from informants represent perceptions, not truths.

The Technology of Fieldwork and Observation

The classic image of the anthropological fieldworker is someone huddled in an African hut writing voluminously by lantern. Evaluation fieldworkers, however, have available to them a number of technological innovations that, when used judiciously, can make fieldwork more efficient and comprehensive. First and foremost are the battery-operated tape recorder and dictaphone. Learning to dictate takes practice, effort, and critical review of early attempts. Tape recorders must be used judiciously so as not to become obtrusive and inhibit social processes or participant responses. A tape recorder is much more useful for recording field notes in private than it is as an instrument to be carried about all time, available to put a quick end to any conversation into which the observer walks.

Portable and compact word processors are another tool that can facilitate the writing of field notes. Photographic materials can also become part of the repertoire of tools available to the fieldworker. Videotape equipment is another technological innovation that has become readily accessible and can sometimes be used unobtrusively.

Whether one uses an instrument of modern technology to take field notes or simply writes down what is occurring, some method of keeping track of observations must be established. In addition, the nature of the recording system must be worked out in accordance with the evaluator's role, the purpose of the observation, and consideration of how the data-gathering process will affect the activities and persons being observed. Many of these procedures and questions must be worked out during the initial phases of fieldwork, the entry period of fieldwork. The next section considers some of the issues that must be addressed during the initial phase of evaluation fieldwork.

The Stages of Fieldwork

Thus far fieldwork has been described as if it was a single, integrated experience. When fieldwork goes well there is a certain continuity to the experience, but it is useful to look at the evolution of fieldwork through identifiable stages. Three stages are worth distinguishing: the entry stage, the basic data-gathering period of fieldwork, and the closing stage.

Entry Into the Program

Entry into the program begins with those who control access to the program. Just because one has approval "from above" in the organization does not mean lower-level staff will cooperate. Nor can client understanding and interest be automatically assumed. Thus entry into the program is a matter for sensitive, diplomatic negotiation. Where the evaluator expects cooperation, gaining entry may be largely a matter of establishing trust and rapport. At the other end of the continuum are those programs where considerable resistance, even hostility, can be expected.

Regardless of how entry is gained, the initial period of observation is likely to remain "the first and most uncomfortable stage of fieldwork" (Wax, 1971, p. 15). It is a time when the observer is getting used to the new setting and the people in that setting are getting used to the observer—a process that has important consequences for the subsequent research.

Anthropologist Rosalie H. Wax (1971) emphasizes the importance of establishing *reciprocal* relationships during entry. This means that while the evaluation observer must learn how to behave in the new setting, the participants in that setting are deciding how to behave toward the observer. Mutual trust, mutual respect, and mutual cooperation depend on the emergence of an exchange relationship in which the evaluator gets data and the people being observed find something that makes their cooperation worthwhile. That something may be feelings of importance from being observed, feedback that helps them improve the program, pleasure from interactions with the observer, or direct assistance in the activities going on in the observational setting. The *reciprocity model* of gaining entry assumes that one can find some reason for participants to cooperate in the evaluation and that some kind of mutual exchange can indeed occur.

Infiltration approaches to entry may become necessary where people are not open to observation, mutual cooperation, and an explicit model of exchange relationships. Douglas (1976, pp. 167-171) has described a number of infiltration strategies, including "worming one's way in," "using the crowbar to pry them open for our observations," showing enough "saintly submissiveness" to make members guilty enough to provide help, or playing the role of a "spineless boob" who could never possibly hurt the people being observed. He has also suggested using various "ploys of indirection" where the researcher diverts people away from the real purpose of the study and convinces them that he is studying something else. There is also the "phased-entree tactic" where the researcher who is refused entree to one group begins by studying another group until it becomes possible to get into the group that is the real focus of the researcher's attention.

For many evaluation situations the best approach to gaining entry may be the *known sponsor approach*. This means that the observer uses the legitimacy and credibility of another person to establish his or her own legitimacy and credibility in the program. When using this approach it is important to make sure that the known sponsor is indeed a source of legitimacy and credibility.

It is well to remember that regardless of the nature of the fieldwork, during the entry stage of fieldwork more than at any other time, *the observer is also the observed.* The evaluator is also being evaluated.

The relative importance of words versus deeds in establishing credibility during entry is partly a function of the length of time the observer expects to be in a setting. For some direct onlooker observations the fieldworker may be present in a particular setting for only a few hours a day. The entry problem in such cases is quite different from the situation where the observer expects to be participating in the activity over some longer period of time. Rosalie Wax described this difference with considerable insight.

> All field workers are concerned about explaining their presence and their work to a host of people. "How shall I introduce myself?" they wonder, or "what shall I say I am doing?"

If the field worker plans to do a very rapid and efficient survey, questions like these are extremely important. The manner in which an interviewer introduces himself, the precise words he uses, may mean the difference between a first-rate job and a failure. . . .

But if the field worker expects to engage in some variety of participant observation, to develop and maintain long-term relationships, to do a study that involves the enlargement of his own understanding, the best thing he can do is relax and remember that most sensible people do not believe what a stranger tells them. In the long run, his host will judge and trust him, not because of what he says about himself or about his research, but by the style in which he lives and acts, the way in which he treats them. In a somewhat shorter run, they will accept or tolerate him because some relative, friend, or person they respect has recommended him to them. (Wax, 1971, p. 365)

Wax argues that over the long run the people being observed will respond to the observer more on the basis of what the observer does than what the observer says about what he or she does. While it is necessary to make some kind of statement about the nature of the evaluation being done, such statements are more a matter of formality and courtesy than they are final determinants of how the evaluator will be received. What the evaluation observer actually does and the kind of relationships the observer establishes with others will determine how people respond to the evaluation and the evaluator.

It is impossible to provide a universal prescription about how to enter programs for evaluation. The nature of the evaluation, the type of program, and the evaluation observer's skills will all affect entry. In selecting a strategy the evaluator will need to use a variety of social skills, psychological sensitivity, and political awareness. The demands on the observer to be sensitive and aware can become so great that this initial period of the observation process can give rise to a great deal of frustration and self-doubt. The fieldworker may lie awake at night worrying about some mistake, some *faux pas,* made during the day. There will be times of embarrassment, of feeling foolish, of feeling uncertain, of questioning the whole purpose of the project, and even of paranoia. The fact that one is a trained evaluation researcher does not mean that one is immune to all the normal pains of learning in and about new situations. But those pains are also part of the data of the study. Moreover, this initial period of fieldwork can also be an exhilarating time, a time of rapid new learning, a time when the senses are heightened by their exposure to new stimuli, and a time of testing one's social, intellectual, emotional, and physical capabilities. The entry stage of fieldwork magnifies both the joys and the pains of using qualitative methods.

Routinization of Fieldwork:
The Social Dynamics of the Second Stage

During the second stage of fieldwork the evaluator has established a role and a purpose and is able to concentrate on and carry out the tasks of gathering data. The observer is no longer caught up in adjustments to the newness of the field setting. The observer begins to really *see* what is going on instead of just looking around.

One of the things that can happen in the course of fieldwork is the emergence of a strong identity with the people being observed. As you come to understand the behaviors, ideals, anxieties, and feelings of participants and staff, you may find yourself identifying with their lives, their hopes, and their worries. Such an identification can be a natural part and a logical consequence of having established relationships of rapport, trust, and mutuality with participants.

To identify, however briefly, with the people in a program can be a startling experience because observers are often quite separated from the observed by education, experience, confidence, and income. Beginning to identify, and be identified, with people being studied creates its own new problems. Social situations are seldom simple. The observer is not immune to the social and political dynamics of the settings being observed. Virtually any setting is likely to include subgroups of people who may be in conflict with other subgroups. These factions or cliques may either woo or reject the observer, but they are seldom neutral.

Indeed, the evaluator may want to become part of a particular program subgroup in order to gain further insight into and understanding of that subgroup. How such an alliance occurs, and how it is interpreted by others, can greatly affect the course of the evaluation. When the evaluation is overt, the observer can sometimes use the responsibilities attached to the position of evaluator to gain access to a faction or clique without becoming part of the subgroup, using as a basis for some distancing the necessity of maintaining basic neutrality for the greater good of the total evaluation process. Any point at which the observer becomes overly identified with a single subgroup, access to other participants may be threatened.

At the same time, it is impractical to expect to have the same degree of closeness to or distance from every group or faction. Evaluators, as human beings with their own personalities and interests, will be naturally attracted to some people more than to others. Indeed, to resist those natural attractions may hinder the observer from acting naturally and being more thoroughly integrated into the setting. Recognizing this, the evaluation observer will be faced with ongoing decisions about personal relationships, group involvement, and how to manage differential associations without losing perspective on what the experience is like for those with whom the evaluator is less directly involved.

While being part of any setting necessarily involves personal choices about social relationships and political choices about group alliances, the emphasis on designing strategies in fieldwork should not be interpreted as suggesting that the conduct of qualitative research in naturalistic settings is an ever-exciting game of chess or war where players and pieces are manipulated to accomplish some ultimate goal. Fieldwork certainly involves times of both exhilaration and frustration, but the dominant motifs in fieldwork are hard work, enormous discipline, and concentration on the mundane, often to the point of boredom. The routinization of fieldwork is a time of concentrated effort and hard work in gathering data.

Bringing Fieldwork to a Close

Over the course of fieldwork, as one nears completion of data-gathering, more and more attention is devoted to matters of interpretation. As the evaluation observer becomes more knowledgeable about the setting being observed, more and more ideas will emerge about things to check out in the program. Possible explanations will have been offered by others; some will have occurred directly to the observer. In short, data analysis has begun, even before leaving the field.

Chapter 6 deals with how the analysis emerges from the data. At this point, it is sufficient to recognize that there is no clear point at which data collection stops and analysis begins. Over the course of the fieldwork one process flows into another. As the observer gains confidence in the field and sophistication about the nature of the program being studied, it is possible to become increasingly analytical about what goes into the field notes.

As fieldwork draws to a close, the evaluator becomes increasingly concerned about *verification* of data, and less concerned with the generation of new data. While the evaluator engaged in naturalistic inquiry avoids imposing preordinate conceptual categories on the people and situations being studied, experience in the field gives rise to categories and dimensions that help organize what has been experienced and observed. These emergent concepts and dimensions generated can also be verified by the fieldwork. Guba (1978) describes this motion back and forth between the discovery mode and the verification mode as a kind of "wave" where the ebb and flow of research involves moving in and out of periods where the investigator is open to new inputs in data and periods where the investigator is testing out hunches, ideas, and explanations.

When fieldwork has gone well the observer grows increasingly confident that things make sense. The evaluator begins to believe in the usefulness and importance of the findings. As fieldwork is coming to an end there will be an increasing integration of data collection and analysis. A holistic conceptual framework should emerge which captures the program's essence. This framework must be understandable and relevant to the stakeholders who will use the findings. The evaluation observer, at this point, comes to believe in her or his own understanding and the usefulness of that understanding for program improvement.

Providing Feedback in the Field

What is also distinct about evaluation research, in contrast to basic science field research, is that the evaluator-observer must also be concerned about feedback. The purpose of evaluation is not simply to publish an academic treatise on the life of the observed. The purpose of program evaluation is to make a difference in decision making and programmatic action. Thus as the fieldwork draws to a close the evaluator-observer must begin to consider how feedback is to be given and to whom, and the nature of the feedback.

The giving of feedback can be a major part of the verification process in fieldwork. My own preference is to provide the participants and staff who have been studied with descriptions and analyses, verbally and informally, and to include their reactions as part of the data. Part of the reciprocity of fieldwork can be an agreement to provide participants with descriptive information about what has been observed. I find that participants and staff are hungry for such information and fascinated by it. I also find that I learn a great deal from their reactions to my descriptions and analyses. Of course, it is not possible to report everything one has observed. Moreover, the informal feedback that occurs at the end of fieldwork is very different from the rigorous analysis that must go on once the investigator leaves the field. But that analysis may take a great deal of time, and while one is still in the field it is possible to share at least some evidence of what the data look like and learn from the reactions of those who are described in the data.

The timing of feedback is particularly important—and difficult—in formative evaluations. When the purpose of the evaluation is to provide data for program improvement, the program staff are often anxious to get that information as soon as possible. In some cases their desire to learn will pressure the evaluator-observer to report findings prematurely before there is reason for confidence in the patterns that have emerged or are emerging.

It is important that evaluators who are providing formative feedback on an ongoing basis not yield to pressures to make interpretations and report analyses before they have confidence that they have observed and sorted out important patterns. Yet there is not necessarily one clear moment in time at which the evaluator-observer knows that he or she now has something to report. The evaluator is caught in a dilemma: Reporting patterns before they are clearly established may lead program staff to intervene to change those patterns inappropriately; on the other hand, giving feedback too late may mean that patterns are so established that they are difficult, if not nearly impossible, to change.

No ideal balance between observing from a distance versus making interpretations and providing feedback has ever emerged for me. Feedback is a matter of judgment and depends on the nature of the relationship between program staff and the evaluator. When in doubt, and where the relationship between the evaluator and program staff has not stabilized into one of long-term trust, I counsel evaluator-observers to err on the side of less feedback rather than more. As often happens in social relationships, negative feedback that was wrong is long remembered and often recounted. On the other hand, it may be a measure of the success of the feedback that program staff so fully adopt it that they make it their own and cease to credit the insights of the evaluator.

Learning how to give feedback in the field is a skill that was not required of the traditional fieldworker. Once feedback is given, the role of the evaluator changes. Those to whom the feedback was presented are likely to become much more conscious of how their behavior and language is being observed. Thus, added to the usual effect of the fieldworker on the setting being observed, this feedback dimension of fieldwork increases the impact of the evaluator-observer on the situation in which he or she is involved.

As the evaluation comes to a close, as the researcher prepares to leave the field, and as he or she organizes notes and thoughts to provide feedback, the impact of that person's presence on the setting may become particularly clear. Providing feedback merely heightens and directs the inevitable effects of having been present in the setting. Because those effects have been of such major concern to people who engage in qualitative methods, the next section considers the question of how the observer affects what is observed.

The Observer and What Is Observed:
Unity and Separation

The problem of how the evaluator affects what is observed is not unique to qualitative evaluation methods. The Heisenberg uncertainty principle in physics expresses the same problem from the perspective of natural science. The Heisenberg uncertainty principle states that the instruments used to measure the velocity and position of an electron alter the accuracy of measurement. When the scientist measures the position of an electron its velocity is changed, and when the focus of measurement is on the velocity, it becomes more difficult to measure accurately its position. The process of observing affects what is observed. These are real effects, not just errors of perception or measurement. The situation is changed by the intrusion of the observer.

Programs are affected by the intrusion of evaluation fieldworkers. How much a program is affected will depend on the nature of the study, the personality and procedures of the observer, and a host of unanticipated conditions. Nor is it simply in fieldwork involving naturalistic inquiry that scientific observers affect what is observed. Experimentalists, survey researchers, cost-benefit analysts, and psychologists who administer standardized tests all affect the situations into which they introduce data collection procedures. The issue is not whether such effects occur. The issue is how to monitor those effects and take them into consideration when interpreting data.

The strength of naturalistic inquiry is that the observer is sufficiently a part of the situation to be able to understand personally what is happening. It is not possible to anticipate exactly how the observer will make a difference. It is possible, when making decisions about what role the observer will play, to anticipate certain of the situations that may arise and to develop strategies for how those situations will be handled. By reviewing the activities that will be going on it is possible to decide to what extent the observer will participate in those activities, and how participation may affect what goes on. Often the role and impact of the observer changes over the course of conducting fieldwork. The fieldwork ideal is a strategy of experiencing the program while at the same time maintaining sufficient mental separation from the program to permit the evaluator to be an observer—to analyze the experience and the program.

Whether one is engaged in participant observation or onlooker observation, what happens in the setting being observed will to some extent depend on the role assumed by the evaluation observer. Likewise, the nature of the data collected will, to some extent, be dependent on the role and perspective of the observer. The personal nature of observations is both their strength and weakness: their strength in that personal involvement permits firsthand experience and understanding, and their weakness in that personal involvement permits the possible introduction of bias and distortion. The interdependence of the observer and what is observed gives naturalistic inquiry its perspective.

Summary Guidelines for Fieldwork

It is difficult, if not impossible, to provide a precise set of rules and procedures for conducting fieldwork. In looking back over this chapter a major theme emerges: What you do depends on the situation, the purpose of the study, the nature of the setting, and the skills, interests, needs, and point of view of the observer. That is indeed the case. Yet there are guidelines for conducting fieldwork:

(1) Be descriptive in taking field notes.
(2) Gather a variety of information from different perspectives.
(3) Cross-validate and triangulate by gathering different kinds of data—observations, interviews, program documentation, recordings, and photographs.
(4) Use quotations; represent program participants in their own terms. Capture participants' views of their experiences in their own words.
(5) Select key informants wisely and use them carefully. Draw on the wisdom of their informed perspectives, but keep in mind that their perspectives are limited.
(6) Be aware of and sensitive to the different stages of fieldwork.
    (a) Build trust and rapport at the entry stage. Remember that the evaluator-observer is also being observed and evaluated.
    (b) Stay alert and disciplined during the more routine middle-phase of fieldwork.
    (c) Focus on pulling together a useful synthesis as fieldwork draws to a close.
    (d) Be disciplined and conscientious in taking detailed field notes at all stages of fieldwork.

(7) Be as involved as possible in experiencing the program as fully as possible while maintaining an analytical perspective grounded in the purpose of the fieldwork: to conduct an evaluation.

(8) Clearly separate description from interpretation and judgment.

(9) Provide formative feedback as part of the verification process of fieldwork. Time that feedback carefully. Observe its impact.

(10) Include in your field notes and evaluation report of your own experiences, thoughts, and feelings. These are also field data.

Fieldwork is a highly personal experience. The meshing of fieldwork procedures with individual capabilities and situational variation is what makes fieldwork a highly personal experience. The validity and meaningfulness of the results obtained depend directly on the evaluation observer's skill, discipline, and perspective. This is both the strength and weakness of observational methods.

Fieldwork is not for everyone. Some, like Henry James, will find that "innocent and infinite are the pleasures of observation." Others find fieldwork anything but pleasurable. Some evaluators have described their experiences to me as tedious, frightening, boring, or "a waste of time." Others have experienced challenge, exhilaration, personal learning, and intellectual insight. More than once the same evaluator has experienced both the tedium and the exhilaration, the fright and the growth, the boredom and the insight.

Observational techniques can be an important part of the methodological repertoire of evaluators, but those techniques are never entirely separate from the individuality of the evaluator doing fieldwork. The observer always puts his or her own mark on the observations, just as the experience of doing fieldwork leaves its mark on the observer.

For Further Reading

Becker, H., & Geer, B. (1970). Participant observation and interviewing: A comparison. In W. J. Filstead (Ed.), *Qualitative methodology.* Chicago: Markham.

Bruyn, S. (1966). *The human perspective in sociology: The methodology of participant observation.* Englewood Cliffs, NJ: Prentice-Hall.

Denzin, N. K. (1978). *The research act.* New York: McGraw-Hill.

Douglas, J. D. (1976). *Investigative social research: Individual and team field research.* Newbury Park, CA: Sage.

Glaser, B. G., & Strauss, A. L. (1976). *Discovery of grounded theory: Strategies for qualitative research.* Chicago: AVC.

Johnson, J. M. (1975). *Doing field research.* New York: Free Press.

Junker, B. H. (1960). *Field work: An introduction to the social sciences.* Chicago: University of Chicago Press.

Lofland, J. (1971). *Analyzing social settings.* Belmont, CA: Wadsworth.

Pelto, P. J., & Pelto, G. H. (1978). *Anthropological research: The structure of inquiry.* Cambridge: Cambridge University Press.

Powdermaker, H. (1966). *Stranger and friend.* New York: Norton.

Wax, R. H. (1971). *Doing fieldwork: Warnings and advice.* Chicago: University of Chicago Press.

Werner, O., & Schoepfle, M. (1987). *Systematic fieldwork* (Vols. 1-2). Newbury Park, CA: Sage.

Chapter 5
Depth Interviewing

Depth interviewing involves asking open-ended questions, listening to and recording the answers, and then following up with additional relevant questions. On the surface this appears to require no more than knowing how to talk and listen. Beneath the surface, however, interviewing becomes an art and science requiring skill, sensitivity, concentration, interpersonal understanding, insight, mental acuity, and discipline.

In ordinary conversations people ask questions and provide answers all the time. But analysis of ordinary conversations will show that there is little depth and much miscommunication. Questions lack clarity. Answers go unheard. The sequence of questions and answers lacks direction. The person asking the question frequently interrupts the person responding. Indeed, one of the greatest obstacles to overcome in learning to be a skilled qualitative interviewer is unlearning the bad habits practiced and reinforced daily in our ordinary conversations.

Depth interviewing is an important source of qualitative data in evaluation. But becoming a skilled interviewer will serve the evaluator well beyond fieldwork. Evaluators need interviewing skills to find out what stakeholders want from an evaluation, to gather information for use in designing a study, and to understand the context for an evaluation. Thus even evaluators who use only or primarily quantitative and experimental methods can benefit from improving their interviewing skills. In working with stakeholders the advice given by Zeno of Citium in 300 B.C. is still highly relevant: "The reason why we have two ears and only one mouth is that we may listen the more and talk the less."

This chapter carries into interviewing the themes of depth, detail, and the search for perspective that are central to all forms of qualitative methods. Depth interviewing probes beneath the surface, soliciting detail and providing a holistic understanding of the interviewee's point of view.

Inner Perspective

Interviewing allows the evaluator to enter another person's world, to understand that person's perspective. The persons interviewed may be program participants, staff, administrators, community members, funders, or officials. In each case the evaluator as interviewer is seeking to find out how that person views the program under study.

Interviews add an inner perspective to outward behaviors. In this way interviews are a source of meaning and elaboration for program observations. We also interview to learn about things we cannot directly observe. We cannot observe everything. We cannot observe feelings, thoughts, and intentions. We cannot observe behaviors that took place at some previous point in time. We cannot observe situations that preclude the presence of an observer. We cannot observe how people have organized the world and the meanings they attach to what goes on in the world. We have to ask people questions about those things. *The purpose of interviewing, then, is to allow us to enter the other person's perspective.*

It is the responsibility of the interviewer to provide a framework within which people can respond comfortably, accurately, and honestly to open-ended questions. The task undertaken by the interviewer is to make it possible for the person being interviewed to bring the interviewer into his or her world. The quality of the information obtained during an interview is largely dependent upon the interviewer. The purpose of this chapter is to discuss ways of obtaining high-quality information by talking with people who have that information.

This chapter begins by discussing three different approaches to qualitative interviewing. Later sections consider the content of interviews: how to ask questions, what to ask questions about, and ways of phrasing depth interview questions. The chapter ends with a discussion of how to record and organize the responses obtained during interviews.

Three Approaches to Qualitative Interviewing

There are three basic approaches to collecting qualitative data through in-depth, open-ended interviews. The three approaches involve different types of preparation, conceptualization, and instrumentation. Each approach has strengths and weaknesses, and each serves a somewhat different purpose. The three choices are: (1) the informal conversational interview, (2) the general interview guide approach, and (3) the standardized open-ended interview.

The difference among these three approaches is the extent to which interview questions are determined and standardized *before* the interview occurs.

The Informal Conversational Interview

The informal conversational interview relies entirely on the spontaneous generation of questions in the natural flow of an interaction, typically an interview that occurs as part of ongoing participant observation fieldwork. During an informal conversational interview, the persons with whom the evaluator is talking may not even realize they are being interviewed. Most of the questions will flow from the immediate context. No predetermined set of questions is possible under such circumstances because the observer does not know beforehand precisely what is going to happen and so does not know what questions will be appropriate.

The data gathered from informal conversational interviews will be different for each person interviewed. In many cases, the same person may be interviewed on a number of different occasions using an informal, conversational approach. This approach is particularly useful where the evaluator can stay in the situation for some period of time, so that he or she is not dependent upon a single interview to collect all the information needed. Interview questions will change over time, and each interview builds on the preceding ones, expanding information that was picked up previously, moving in new directions, seeking elucidations and elaborations from various participants in their own terms. The interviewer must "go with the flow."

The strength of the informal conversational approach to interviewing is that it allows the interviewer to be highly responsive to individual differences and situational changes. Questions can be individualized to establish in-depth communication with the person being interviewed and to make use of the immediate surroundings and situation to increase the concreteness and immediacy of the interview questions and responses.

The weakness of the informal conversational interview is that it requires a great amount of time to get systematic information. It may take several conversations with different people before a similar set of questions has been posed to several respondents. The informal conversational interview is also more open to interviewer effects in that it depends upon the conversational skills of the interviewer to a greater extent than do more formal, standardized formats. The conversational interviewer must be able to interact easily with people in a variety of settings, must be able to generate rapid insights, to formulate questions quickly and smoothly, and to guard against asking questions that impose interpretations on the situation by the structure of the questions. Data obtained from informal conversational interviews are also difficult to pull together and analyze. Because different questions will generate different responses, the interviewer has to spend a great deal of time sifting through responses to find patterns that have emerged at different points in different interviews with different people. By contrast, interviews that are more systematized and standardized facilitate analysis but are less responsive to individual and situational differences.

The Interview Guide

An interview guide is a list of questions or issues that are to be explored in the course of an interview. An interview guide is prepared to make sure that essentially the same information is obtained from a number of people by covering the same material. The interview guide provides topics or subject areas about which the interviewer is free to explore, probe, and ask questions that will elucidate and illuminate that particular subject. The issues in the outline need not be taken in any particular order and the actual working of questions to elicit responses about those issues is not determined in advance. The interview guide simply serves as a basic checklist during the interview to make sure that all relevant topics are covered. The interviewer is thus required to adapt both the wording and sequence of questions to specific respondents in the context of the actual interview. The interviewer remains free to build a conversation within a particular subject area, to word questions spontaneously, and to establish a conversational style— but with the focus on a particular predetermined subject.

The advantage of an interview guide is that it makes sure the interviewer has carefully decided how best to use the limited time available in an interview situation. The interview guide helps make interviewing different people more systematic and comprehensive by delimiting the issues to be discussed in the interview. The interview guide approach is especially useful in conducting group interviews. A guide keeps the interaction focused, but allows individual perspectives and experiences to emerge.

Interview guides can be developed in more or less detail, depending on the extent to which the evaluator is able to specify important issues in advance and the extent to which it is important to ask questions in the same order to all respondents. What follows is an example of an interview guide used with participants in a manpower training program.

Interview Guide for
Manpower Program Evaluation

What has the trainee done in the program—activities? interactions? products? work performed?

What are the trainee's current work skills? What things can the trainee do that are marketable?

How has the trainee been affected by the program in areas other than job skills—feelings about self? attitudes toward work? aspirations? interpersonal skills? spinoffs?

What are the trainee's plans for the future—work plans? income expectations? life-style expectations/plans?

What does the trainee think of the program—strengths? weaknesses? things liked? things disliked? best components? poor components? things that should be changed? (Patton, 1980b, p. 201)

This interview guide provides a framework within which the interviewer would develop questions, sequence those questions, and make decisions about which information to pursue in greater depth. The interviewer would normally not be expected to go into totally new subjects that are not covered within the framework of the interview guide. The interviewer does not ask questions, for example, about previous employment or education, how the person got into the program, how this program compares with other programs the trainee has experienced, and the trainee's health.

The flexibility permitted by the interview guide approach will become clearer after reviewing the third strategy of qualitative interviewing.

The Standardized Open-Ended Interview

The *standardized open-ended interview* consists of a set of questions carefully worded and arranged for the purpose of taking each respondent through the same sequence and asking each respondent the same questions with essentially the same words. Flexibility in probing is more or less limited, depending on the nature of the interview and the skills of interviewers. The standardized, open-ended interview is used when it is important to minimize variation in the questions posed to interviewees. This reduces the bias that can occur from having different interviews for different people, including the problem of obtaining a great deal of data from certain persons while getting less systematic information from others.

A standardized open-ended interview may be particularly appropriate when several people are to conduct interviews and the evaluator wishes to reduce the variation in responses due purely to the fact that, left to themselves, different interviewers will ask questions on the same topic in different ways. By controlling and standardizing the open-ended interview the investigator obtains data that are systematic and thorough for each respondent, but flexibility and spontaneity are considerably reduced.

In many evaluations it is only possible to interview participants for a very limited period of time. Sometimes it is only possible to interview each participant once. At other times it is possible and desirable to interview participants before they enter an experience, when they leave the experience, and again after some period of time (e.g., six months) has elapsed since they completed the experience. Because of limited time, and because it is desirable to have the same information from each person interviewed, a standardized open-ended format may be used. The interview questions are written in advance *exactly* the way they are to be asked during the interview. Careful consideration is given to the wording of each question before the interview. Any clarifications or elaborations that are to be used are written into the interview itself. Probing questions are placed in the interview at appropriate places.

The basic purpose of the standardized open-ended interview is to minimize interviewer effects by asking the same question of each respondent. Because the interview is systematic, interviewer judgment during the interview is reduced. The standardized open-ended interview also makes data analysis easier because it is possible to locate each respondent's answer to the same question rather quickly, and to organize questions and answers that are similar. In addition, by generating a standardized form, other evaluators can more easily replicate a study in new programs, using the same interview instrument with different subjects. Future researchers will then know exactly what was, and was not, previously asked.

The standardized open-ended interview also reduces variation among interviewers. Some studies use volunteers to do interviewing; in other instances interviewers may be novices, students, or others who are not professional social scientists. When a number of different interviewers are used, variations in data created by differences among interviewers will become particularly apparent if an informal conversational approach to data-gathering is used or even if each interviewer uses a basic guide. The best way to guard against variations among interviewers is to word questions carefully in advance and train the interviewers to stick with the interview. The data collected are still open-ended in the sense that the respondent supplies his or her own words, thoughts, and insights in answering the questions, but the precise wording of the questions is predetermined.

The weakness of this approach is that it restricts the pursuit of topics or issues that were not anticipated when the interview was written. Constraints are also placed on the use of different lines of questioning with different people based on their unique experiences. Therefore, a standardized open-ended interview approach will reduce the extent to which individual differences and circumstances can be taken into account.

Style Combinations

It is possible to combine an informal conversational approach with an interview guide approach. It is also possible to combine an interview guide approach with a standardized open-ended approach. For example, a number of basic questions may be worded quite precisely in a predetermined fashion, while permitting the interviewer more flexibility in probing and considerable freedom in determining when it is appropriate to explore certain subjects in greater depth, or even to undertake whole new areas of inquiry that were not originally included in the interview instrument. It is even possible to have a standardized open-ended interview format for the early part of an interview and then to leave the interviewer free to pursue any subjects of interest during the latter parts of the interview. Another combination would include using the informal conversational interview early in the evaluation followed midway by an interview guide and then closing the study with a standardized open-ended interview to provide systematic information from a sample of subjects at the end of the experience or when conducting follow-up of participants.

Summary of Interviewing Strategies

The common characteristic of all three qualitative approaches to depth interviewing is that the persons being interviewed respond in their own words to express their own personal perspectives. While there are variations in strategy concerning the extent to which the wording and sequencing of questions ought to be predetermined, there is no variation in the principle that the response format should be open-ended. The interviewer never supplies and predetermines the phrases or categories that must be used by respondents to express themselves. The purpose of qualitative interviewing in evaluation is to understand how people in a program view the program, to learn their terminology and judgments, and to capture the complexities of their individual perceptions and experiences. This is what distinguishes qualitative interviewing from the closed interview, questionnaire, or test typically used in quantitative research. Such closed instruments force respondents to fit their knowledge, experiences, and feelings into the evaluator's categories. *The fundamental principle of qualitative interviewing is to provide a framework within which respondents can express their own understandings in their own terms.* Table 5.1 summarizes the basic variations in evaluation research interview instrumentation. In reviewing this summary table it is important to keep in mind that these are presented as pure types. In practice any particular study may employ several of these strategies or combinations of approaches.

The Content of Interviews: What Questions to Ask

A number of decisions must be made in conceptualizing an interview, whether the interview takes place spontaneously in the field or is carefully prepared as a standardized open-ended instrument. The evaluator must decide what questions to ask, how to sequence questions, how much detail to solicit, how long to make the interview, and how to word the actual questions. These are all measurement questions that will affect the quality of interview responses.

There are basically six kinds of questions that can be asked of people. It is possible to ask any of these questions on any given topic.

Experience/Behavior Questions

These are questions about what a person does or has done. These questions are aimed at eliciting descriptions of experiences, behaviors, actions, and activities that would have been observable had the observer been present. "If I had been in the program with you, what would I have seen you doing?" "If I followed you through a typical day, what would I see you doing, what experiences would I observe you having?"

TABLE 5.1
Variations in Evaluation Research Interview Instrumentation

Type of Interview	Characteristics	Strengths	Weaknesses
(1) Informal conversational interview	Questions emerge from the immediate context and are asked in the natural course of things; there is no predetermination of question topics or wording.	Increases the salience and relevance of questions; interviews are built on and emerge from observations; the interview can be matched to individuals and circumstances.	Different information collected from different people with different questions. Less systematic and comprehensive if certain questions do not arise "naturally." Data organization and analysis can be quite difficult.
(2) Interview guide approach	Topics and issues to be covered are specified in advance, in outline form; interviewer decides sequence and wording of questions in the course of the interview.	The outline increases the comprehensiveness of the data and makes data collection somewhat systematic for each respondent. Logical gaps in data can be anticipated and closed. Interviews remain fairly conversational and situational.	Important and salient topics maybe inadvertently omitted. Interviewer flexibility in sequencing and wording questions can result in substantially different respondents, thus reducing the comparability of responses.

| (3) Standardized open-ended interview | The exact wording and sequence of questions are determined in advance. All interviewees are asked the same basic questions in the same order. | Respondents answer the same questions, thus increasing comparability of responses; data are complete for each person on the topics addressed in the interview. Reduces interviewer effects and bias when several interviewers are used. Permits decision makers to see and review the instrumentation used in the evaluation. Facilitates organization and analysis of the data. | Little flexibility in relating the interview to particular individuals and circumstances; standardized wording of questions may constrain and limit naturalness and relevance of questions and answers. |
| (4) Closed quantitative interview | Questions and response categories are determined in advance. Responses are fixed; respondent chooses from among these fixed responses. | Data analysis is simple; responses can be directly compared and easily aggregated; many questions can be asked in a short time. | Respondents must fit their experiences and feelings into the researcher's categories; may be perceived as impersonal, irrelevant, and mechanistic. Can distort what respondents really mean or experienced by so completely limiting their response choices. |

Opinion/Belief Questions

These are questions aimed at understanding the cognitive and interpretive processes of people. Answers to these questions tell us what people *think* about the world or about a specific setting. They tell us about people's goals, intentions, desires, and values. These questions typically carry an implication of respondent rationality and decision making. "What do you believe?" "What do you think?" "What would you like to see happen?" "What is your opinion of _____?"

Feeling Questions

These are questions aimed at understanding the emotional responses of people to their experiences and thoughts. There is an implicit assumption of spontaneity about the origin of emotional responses. Feelings occur inside people. They are their natural, emotional responses to what happens around them or to them. Feelings tap the affective dimension of human life. In asking feeling questions, the interviewer is looking for "adjective responses" (e.g., feeling anxious, happy, afraid, intimidated, confident).

Opinions and feelings are often confused. It is critical that interviewers understand the distinction between the two, in order to know when they have the kind of answer they want to the question they are asking. Suppose an interviewer asks, "How do you feel about that?" The response is "I think it's probably the best that we can do under the circumstances." The question about *feelings* has not really been answered. Analytical, interpretive, and opinion statements are not answers to questions about feelings.

This confusion sometimes occurs because interviewers give the wrong cues when asking questions, for example, by asking opinion questions using the format "How do you feel about that?" instead of "What is your opinion about that" or "What do you think about it?" When you want to understand the respondent's emotional reactions it is appropriate to ask about feelings. When you want to understand what they think about something, the question should explicitly ask about opinions, beliefs, and considered judgments—not about feelings.

Knowledge Questions

Knowledge questions are aimed at finding out what factual information the respondent has. The assumption here is that certain things are considered to be *known*. These things are not opinions, they are not feelings, but rather they are the things that one *knows*. They are the facts of the case. Knowledge about a social program may consist of reporting on what services are available, who is eligible, the characteristics of clients, who the program serves, how long people spend in the program, what the rules and regulations of the program are, how one enrolls in the program, and so on. While from a philosophical point of view it is possible to argue that all knowledge is merely a set of beliefs rather than facts, the issue here is to find out what the person being interviewed considers to be factual. It is the respondent's knowledge about the program and the world that is being elicited.

Sensory Questions

These are questions about what is seen, heard, touched, tasted, and smelled. The purpose of these questions is to allow the interviewer to enter into the sensory apparatus of the respondent. "When you walk through the doors of your mother's house, what do you see? Describe to me what I would see if I walked into your mother's house." Or again, "What does the counselor ask you when you meet with him? What does he actually say?" Sensory questions attempt to have the interviewee describe the stimuli to which he or she is subject.

Background/Demographic Questions

These questions concern the identifying characteristics of the person being interviewed. Answers to these questions help you locate the respondent in relation to other people. Age, education, occupation, residence, income, time in program, and the like are standard topics for background questions. They are distinguishable from knowledge questions primarily by their routine nature.

Questions about behaviors, opinions, feelings, knowledge, sensations, or demographics: These are the kinds of questions that it is possible to ask in an interview. Any kind of question one might want to ask can be subsumed in one of these categories. Keeping these types of questions in mind can be particularly helpful when it comes to planning the comprehensiveness of the interview and ordering the questions in some sequence.

The Time Frame of Questions

Any of the questions described above can be asked in the present tense, past tense, or future tense. For example, it is possible to ask a person what they are doing now, what they have done in the past, and what they plan to do in the future. Likewise, one might be interested in present attitudes, past attitudes, or future attitudes. By combining the time frame of questions with the different types of questions it is possible to construct a matrix which generates eighteen different types of questions. Table 5.2 shows that matrix.

Asking all eighteen questions about any particular situation, event, or programmatic activity may become somewhat tedious, especially if the sequence is repeated over and over throughout the interview for different subjects. The matrix constitutes a set of options from which one can select the pieces of information that are most important to obtain.

Sequencing the Questions

There are no fixed rules of sequence in organizing an interview. Informal conversational interviewing is flexible and responsive so that a fixed sequence is seldom possible. However, standardized open-ended interviews must establish a fixed sequence of questions due to their structured format. I offer, then, some suggestions about sequencing.

I prefer to begin the interview with questions about noncontroversial present behaviors, activities, and experiences. Such questions ask for relatively straightforward descriptions; they require minimal recall and interpretation. Such questions are therefore fairly easy to answer. They encourage the respondent to talk descriptively. Probes should focus on eliciting greater detail, filling out the descriptive picture.

Once some experience or activity has been described it is appropriate to ask about interpretations, opinions, and feelings about the behaviors and actions described. Opinions and feelings are likely to be more accurate at this point in the interview because the respondent has just verbally relived the experience. Thus a context is established for expressing feelings and opinions.

Knowledge and skill questions also typically need a context. These questions can be quite threatening. It is helpful to ask them in conjunction with specific questions about program activities and experiences that have a bearing on knowledge and skills. Finding out from people what they know and what skills they possess works best once some rapport and trust have been established in the interview. Relating knowledge and skills to descriptions of program activity can help provide a concrete context for these kinds of questions.

TABLE 5.2
A Matrix of Question Options

	Past	*Present*	*Future*
Behavior/experience questions			
Opinion/value questions			
Feeling questions			
Knowledge questions			
Sensory questions			
Demographic/background questions			

Questions about the present tend to be easier for respondents than questions about the future. Future-oriented questions involve considerable speculation, and responses to questions about future actions or attitudes are typically less reliable than questions about the present or past. I generally prefer to begin by asking questions about the present, then, using the present as a baseline, ask questions about the same activity or attitude in the past. Only then will I broach questions about the future.

Background and demographic questions are basically boring; they epitomize what people do not like about interviews. They can also be somewhat uncomfortable for the respondent, depending on how personal they are. I keep such questions to an absolute minimum and prefer to space them strategically and unobtrusively throughout the interview. I advise never beginning an interview with a long list of routine demographic questions. In qualitative interviewing the interviewee needs to become actively involved in providing descriptive information as soon as possible instead of becoming conditioned to providing short-answer, routine responses to uninteresting categorical questions. Some background information may be necessary at the beginning to make sense out of the rest of the interview, but such questions should be tied to descriptive information about present program experience as much as possible. Otherwise, save the sociological-demographic inquiries (age, socieoconomic status, birth order, and the like) for the end.

The Wording of Questions

An interview question is a stimulus that is aimed at creating or generating a response from the person being interviewed. The way a question is worded is one of the most important elements in determining how the interviewee will respond. As Stanley L. Payne (1951) put it, asking questions is an art. For purposes of qualitative evaluation, good questions should, at a minimum, be open-ended, neutral, sensitive, and clear. Each of these criteria will be discussed below.

Asking Truly Open-Ended Questions

The basic thrust of qualitative interviewing is to minimize the imposition of predetermined responses when gathering data. When using qualitative interviewing strategies for data collection it is critical that questions be asked in a truly open-ended fashion. This means that the question should permit the person being interviewed to respond in his or her own terms.

The standard questionnaire item in quantitative measurement provides the respondent with a categorical list of response possibilities.

> How do you feel about the program? Would you say that you are (a) very satisfied, (b) somewhat satisfied, (c) not too satisfied, (d) not at all satisfied.

It is clear in this instance that the question is closed and that the respondent has been provided with a limited and predetermined set of alternatives. The response possibilities are clearly stated and made *explicit* in the way in which the question is asked. Many interviewers think that the way to make a question open-ended is simply to leave out the structured response categories. Such an approach does *not*, however, make a question truly open-ended. It merely makes the predetermined response categories implicit and disguised. Consider the following "open-ended" question:

> How satisfied are you with this program?

On the surface this appears to be an open-ended question. On close inspection, however, it is clear that the dimension along which the respondent can answer the question has already been identified. The respondent is being asked for some degree of satisfaction. It is true that the interviewee can use a variety of modifiers for the word satisfaction, such as "pretty satisfied," "kind of satisfied," "mostly satisfied." But in effect the response set has been narrowly limited by the wording of the question. The desired dimension of response is identified in the wording of the question such that the typical answers are only slightly different from those that would have been obtained had the categories been standardized and closed.

The truly open-ended question does not presuppose which dimensions of feeling, analysis, or thought will be salient for the interviewee. The truly open-ended question allows the person being interviewed to select from among that person's full repertoire of possible responses. Indeed, in qualitative interviewing one of the things the evaluator is trying to determine is what dimensions, themes, and images or words people use among themselves to describe their feelings, thoughts, and experiences. Truly open-ended questions would follow this format:

> How do you feel about the program?
> What is your opinion of the program?
> What do you think about the program?

The truly open-ended question permits the persons being interviewed to take whatever direction and use whatever words they want.

Asking Clear Questions

It is the responsibility of the interviewer to make it clear to the interviewee what is being asked. Asking questions that are understandable is an important part of establishing rapport. Unclear questions can make the person being interviewed feel uncomfortable, ignorant, confused, or hostile. Asking focused questions helps a great deal to make things clear. There are a number of other factors which contribute to clarity.

In preparing to do an interview, find out what language the people you are interviewing use in talking about the program being studied. Use language that is understandable and part of the frame of reference of the person being interviewed. During the interview pay attention to what language the respondent uses to describe the setting, program participants, special activities, or whatever else is reported. The interviewer then uses the language provided by the interviewee in the rest of the interview. Questions which use the respondent's own language are questions which are most likely to be *clear* to the respondent.

Being clear about what you are asking contributes to the process of establishing and maintaining rapport during an interview. Using words that make sense to the interviewee, words that are sensitive to the respondent's context and world view, will improve the quality of data obtained during the interview.

Asking Singular Questions

It is widely understood that questionnaire items should be clear, specific, and singular. Yet, when doing depth interviews many people think there is no longer any reason for precision. Interviewers often throw several questions together and ask them all at once, usually because they are not clear about what they want to ask. This is confusing and places an unnecessary and unfair burden of interpretation on the interviewee. Consider this question:

> In order to help the staff improve the program, we'd like to ask you to talk about your opinion of the program. What do you think are the strengths and weaknesses of the program? What do you like? What don't you like? What do you think could be improved or should stay the same?

This sequence asks far too much. Reflection on the strengths and weaknesses of a program is not the same as reporting on what one likes and dislikes. Likewise, recommendations for change may not be directly linked in the mind of the respondent to specific strengths, weaknesses, likes, and dislikes.

It can be helpful to alert the interviewee to a series of related questions, but then each should be asked in order.

> Now I'd like to ask you to reflect on the program's strengths and weaknesses, then to suggest possible improvements and changes. First, then, what do you consider the program's strengths?
>
> [Interviewee responds.]
>
> OK, what about weaknesses?
>
> [Interviewee responds.]
>
> What changes would you recommend to improve the program?
>
> [Interviewee responds.]

In summary, ask clear and precise, yet genuinely open-ended questions. Know what you want to find out and ask one question at a time.

Probes and Follow-Up Questions

Probes are used to deepen the response to a question, to increase the richness of the data being obtained, and to give cues to the interviewee about the level of response that is desired. The word "probe" itself is usually best avoided in interviews. "Let me probe that further" may sound like you are about to perform surgery on the respondent or are conducting an investigation of something illicit or illegal. Quite simply, a probe is an interview technique used to go deeper into the interview responses. As such, probes should be conversational, offered in a natural style and voice, and used to follow-up initial responses.

One natural set of conversational probes consists of *detail-oriented* questions. These are the basic questions that fill in the blank spaces of a response.

> When did that happen?
> Who else was involved?
> Where were you during that time?
> What was your involvement in that situation?
> How did that come about?
> Where did that happen?

These *detail-oriented* probes are the basic "who," "where," "what," "when," and "how" questions that are used to get a complete and detailed picture of some activity or experience. There are times, as in the probes suggested above, when *particular* details are elicited through follow-up questions. At other times an interviewer wants to keep a respondent talking more about a subject. In such cases *elaboration* probes are used. Elaboration probes encompass a variety of ways to cue the person being interviewed that you'd like them to keep talking.

There are times when you want the interviewee to say more because you have not fully understood an answer. If something has been said that is unclear, ambiguous, or an apparent non sequitur, a *clarification* probe may be useful. Clarification probes tell the interviewee that you need more information, or a restatement of the answer, or more context. A clarification probe should be used quite naturally and gently. It is best for the interviewer to convey the notion that the failure to understand is the "fault" of the interviewer and not a failure by the person being interviewed. The interviewer does not want to make the respondent feel inarticulate, stupid, or muddled. After one or two attempts at achieving clarification, it is sometimes best to leave the particular topic that is causing the confusion and move on to other questions, perhaps returning to that topic at a later point.

A major characteristic that separates probes from general interview questions is that probes are seldom written out in an interview. Probing is an art and skill that comes from knowing what you are looking for in the interview, listening carefully to what is and is not said, and being sensitive to the feedback needs of the person being interviewed. Probes are always a combination of verbal and nonverbal cues. Silence at the end of a response can indicate as effectively as anything else that you would like the person to continue. Probes are used to communicate with the interviewee about what you, the interviewer, want—more detail? elaboration? more clarity? Probes, then, provide guidance to the person being interviewed. They also provide the interviewer with a way to maintain control of the flow of the interview, a subject discussed in more detail in a later section.

Support and Recognition Responses

Effective interviewing feels to both the interviewer and the interviewee like genuine two-way communication. Interviews should not be interrogations where the interviewer intensively pursues a set of questions and the respondent provides the answers. The interviewer has a responsibility to communicate clearly about what information is desired, why that information is important, and to let the interviewee know how the interview is progressing. These things constitute the interviewer's communication to the person being interviewed.

Previous sections have emphasized wording questions for clarity and probing for detailed responses. The purpose of the overall interview and the relationship of particular questions to that overall purpose are important pieces of information that go beyond the simple asking of questions. While the reason for asking a particular question may be absolutely clear to the interviewer, it may not be clear to the respondent. The interviewer communicates respect for people being interviewed by giving them the courtesy of explaining why questions are being asked. Understanding the purpose of the interview will increase the interviewee's motivation to respond openly and in detail.

The other part of this process of maintaining communication with the interviewee is giving out clues about how the interview is going. One of the most common mistakes in interviewing is a failure to provide reinforcement and feedback to the person being interviewed about how the interviewer perceives the interview progressing. This means that it is necessary, from time to time, to let the interviewee know that the purpose of the interview is being fulfilled. Words of thanks, support, and praise will help make the interviewee feel that the interview process is worthwhile. Here are some examples:

It's really helpful to get such a clear statement of what this community is like. That's just the kind of thing we're trying to get at.

We are about half-way through the interview now and I think a lot of really important things are coming out of what you're saying.

I really appreciate your willingness to express your feelings about that. That's very helpful.

The point here is that the interview is an interaction. The interviewer provides stimuli to generate a reaction. That reaction from the interviewee, however, is also a stimulus to which the interviewer responds. The flow of communication back and forth occurs in the context of the whole interaction. The interviewer must maintain awareness of how the interview is flowing, how the interviewee is reacting to questions, and what kinds of feedback are appropriate and helpful to maintain the flow of the interview.

Neutrality and Rapport

As an interviewer I want to establish rapport with the person I am questioning, but establishing that rapport must not undermine my neutrality concerning what the person tells me. Neutrality means that the interviewer listens without passing judgment. I can be told anything without reacting with either favor or disfavor to the content of what I am told. I cannot be shocked; I cannot be angered; I cannot be embarrassed; I cannot be saddened; indeed, nothing people tell me will make me think more or less of them. In short, I am neutral about the content of their responses.

However, while I am neutral with regard to the *content* of what I am told, I care very much that this person is willing to share with me what she or he is saying. *Rapport is a stance vis-à-vis the person being interviewed. Neutrality is a stance vis-à-vis the content of what that person says.* Rapport means that I respect the person being interviewed, so what that person says is terribly important because of who is saying it. I want to convey that the respondent's knowledge, experiences, attitudes, and feelings are important. Yet the content of what I am told will not be subject to my judgment one way or the other.

Questions to Communicate Neutrality

One kind of question wording that can help establish neutrality is the *illustrative examples* format. When phrasing questions in this way I want to let the person I am interviewing know that I have pretty much heard it all. I've heard the bad things and I've heard the good things and so I'm not interested in something that's particularly sensational, particularly negative, or especially positive. I am really only interested in what that person's experience has really been like. An example of the illustrative examples format is provided by a question taken from interviews we conducted with juvenile delinquents who has been placed in foster group homes. One section of the interview was aimed at finding out how the juveniles were treated by group home parents.

> OK, now I'd like to ask you to tell me how you were treated in the group home by the parents. Some kids have told us that they felt they were treated like one of the family in the group home; some kids have told us that they got knocked around and beat up by the group home parents; some kids have told us about sexual things that were done to them; some of the kids have told us about recreation and hobby kinds of things; some of the kids have felt they were treated really well and some kids have felt they were treated really bad. When you think about how *you* were treated in the group home, what kinds of things come to mind?

A closely related kind of format is the *illustrative extremes* format. With this format I attempt to let the interviewee know that I've heard it all by giving examples only of extreme kinds of responses.

> How much dope did you use while you were in the group home? Some kids have told me they were doped up the whole time they were in the home, they smoked or dropped stuff every day and every night, while other kids have said that they decided to stay completely straight while they were in the home. How about you?

In both the illustrative examples format and the illustrative extremes format it is critical to avoid asking a *leading* question. Leading questions are the opposite of neutral questions. Leading questions give the interviewee hints about what would be a desirable or appropriate kind of answer. Leading questions "lead" the respondent in a certain direction. This is an example of a typical leading question that might be asked of juveniles:

> We know that most kids use a lot of dope because that's part of what it means to be young, so we figure you use it too—right? So what do you think about everybody using dope?

This question has a built-in response bias that communicates the interviewer's belief that drug use among the young is legitimate and universal. The question is "leading" because the interviewee is led into acquiescence with the interviewer's point of view.

It is important in giving examples during an interview that the examples cover several dimensions and are balanced between what might be construed as positive and negative kinds of responses. My own preference is to use these illustrative formats only as clarifying questions after having begun with a simple, straightforward, and truly open-ended question where the response was not constrained or influenced by any kinds of examples: "What has been your experience with the use of drugs in the group home?"

Sensitivity

It is the interviewer's responsibility to be sensitive to how the interviewee may be affected by different questions and various question formats. It is not possible here to review all possible variations on how to ask questions. A few examples of sensitive question formats are provided here to illustrate the point that *how* the question is worded can make a great deal of difference in the quality of the response received.

One stylistic technique that shows sensitivity to the interviewee is providing a context for a question. This can have the effect of making a particularly probing question less personal and intrusive. Consider the two questions below:

How do inmates sneak dope into the prison?

[versus]

Suppose someone you trusted asked you how inmates sneak dope into the prison, what would you tell him?

The first question comes across like an interrogation or inquisition. The second question is softened, and has more of an informal and sensitive tone to it. Despite the fact that content is the same for both questions, the second question has the psychological effect on the interviewee of permitting the interviewer to be dissociated from the question. While this technique can be overused and can come across as a phony or trick question if the intonation with which it is asked is hesitating or implies awkwardness, used sparingly and with subtlety this format can ease the asking of difficult questions and can permit the interviewer to obtain high-quality information.

Simulation questions provide context in a different way. The simulation question asks the person being interviewed to imagine himself or herself in some situation about which the interviewer is interested.

> Suppose I was present with you during one of your group therapy sessions. What would I see happening? What would be going on? Describe to me what one of those sessions is like.

In effect, these kinds of questions ask the interviewee to become an observer. The observer is asked to simulate for the interviewer some situation that has been experienced. In most cases, a response to this question will require the interviewee to visualize in his or her head the situation to be described. When the interviewee is able to move fully into an experience of the simulated situation through a visualization, the interviewer may observe that the person being interviewed takes on a faraway expression as if they are someplace else. They are. That's the point of the question. Do not try to bring them back, but rather encourage them to describe to you what is happening in the simulation. I frequently find that the richest and most detailed descriptions come from a series of questions that ask a respondent to re-experience and/or simulate some experience.

Maintaining Control of the Interview

Time is precious in an interview. Long-winded responses, irrelevant remarks, and getting sidetracked in the interview will reduce the amount of time available for focusing on critical questions. This means that the interviewer must maintain control of the interview. Control is maintained by (1) knowing what it is you want to find out, (2) asking the right questions to get the information you need, and (3) giving appropriate verbal and nonverbal feedback.

Knowing what information you need means being able to recognize and distinguish appropriate from inappropriate responses. It is not enough just to ask the right questions. The interviewer must listen carefully to make sure that the responses received provide answers to the questions that are asked. Consider the following exchange:

> Interviewer: What happens in a typical interviewer training session that you lead?
>
> Respondent: I try to be sensitive to where each person is at with interviewing. I try to make sure that I am able to touch base with each person so that I

can find out how they're responding to their training, to get some notion of how each person is doing.

Interviewer: How do you begin a session, a training session?

Respondent: I believe it's important to begin with enthusiasm, to generate some excitement about interviewing.

In this interaction the interviewer is asking descriptive, behavioral questions. The responses, however, are about beliefs and hopes. The responses do not actually describe what happened. Rather, the responses describe what the interviewee thinks ought to happen. Since the interviewer wants descriptive data, it is necessary to first recognize that the responses are not providing the kind of data desired, and then to ask appropriate questions that will lead to behavioral responses.

Interviewer: OK, you try to establish contact with each person, and you try to generate enthusiasm at the beginning. What I'd like you to do now is to actually take me to a training session. Describe for me what the room looks like, where the trainees are, where you are, and tell me what I would see and hear if I were right there in that session. What would I see you doing? What would I hear you saying? What would I see the trainees doing? Take me into a session so that I can actually experience it.

It is the interviewer's responsibility to work with the person being interviewed to facilitate the desired responses. At times it may be necessary to give more direct feedback about the kind of information that has been received and the kind of information that is desired.

Interviewer: I think I understand now what it is you try to do during an interview training session. You've explained to me what you hope to accomplish and stimulate, now I'd like you to describe to me what you actually do, not what you expect, but what I would actually see happening if I was present at the session.

It is not enough to simply ask the right initial question. Neither is it enough to have a well-planned interview with good, on-target basic questions. The interviewer must listen carefully to the kinds of responses supplied to make sure that the interview is working according to plan. I've seen many well-written interviews that have resulted in largely useless data because the interviewer did not listen carefully to the responses being received and did not recognize that the responses were not providing the kind of information needed. The first responsibility, then, in maintaining control of the interview is knowing what kind of data one is looking for and directing the interview in order to collect that data.

Giving appropriate feedback to the interviewee is essential in pacing an interview and maintaining control of the interview process. Head nodding, taking notes, "uh-huhs," and silent probes (remaining quiet when a person stops talking) are all signals about how the interview is progressing. On the other hand, it is often necessary to stop a highly verbal respondent who gets off the track. The first step in stopping the long-winded respondent is to cease giving the usual cues mentioned above that encourage talking: Stop nodding the head; interject a new question as soon as the respondent pauses for breath; stop taking notes, or call attention to the fact that you've stopped taking notes by flipping the page of the writing pad and sitting back, waiting. When these nonverbal cues do not work, it becomes necessary to interrupt the long-winded respondent.

> Let me stop you here, for a moment. I want to make sure I fully understand something you said earlier. (Then ask a question aimed at getting the more targeted response.)
>
> [or]
>
> Let me ask you to stop for a moment because some of what you're talking about now I want to get later in the interview. First I need to find out from you . . .

Interviewers are sometimes concerned that it is impolite to interrupt an interviewee. It certainly can be awkward, but when done with respect and sensitivity, the interruption can actually help the interview. It is both patronizing and disrespectful to let the respondent run on when no attention is being paid to what he or she is saying. It is respectful of both the person being interviewed and the interviewer to make good use of the short time available to talk. It is the responsibility of the interviewer to help the interviewee understand what kind of information is being requested and to establish a framework and context that makes it possible to collect the right kind of information.

One example of how this can be done is to tell the interviewee quite explicitly that you, as the interviewer, may have to interrupt a response to keep the interview moving along so that all questions are covered in the time available. This announcement about the interviewer's role will help legitimate subsequent interruptions. Thus I might say something like the following:

> Excuse me a moment here. Let me interrupt at this point to be sure I'm following you. I find myself feeling very conscious of how many questions I still need to ask you, and how quickly interview time can pass. What I'd like

to do is move on through the next sections of the interview, and then come back to fill in more detail if we have time at the end. I'm anxious to get your responses to all the questions, so I hope you'll forgive me if I interrupt some of your more detailed responses and hold those for later. Okay, the next question I'd like to ask is . . .

Asking focused questions in an appropriate style to get relevant answers that are useful in understanding the interviewee's world is what interviewing is all about. Yet maintaining focus on information that is useful, relevant, and appropriate requires concentration, practice, and the ability to separate that which is foolish from that which is important. In his classic *Don Quixote* Cervantes describes a scene in which Sancho is rebuked by Don Quixote for trying to impress his cousin by repeating deeply philosophical questions and answers that he has heard from other people, all the while trying to make the cousin think that these philosophical discourses were Sancho's own insights.

"That question and answer," said Don Quixote, "are not yours, Sancho. You have heard them from someone else." "Whist, sir," answered Sancho, "if I start questioning and answering, I shan't be done til tomorrow morning. Yes, for if it's just a matter of asking idiotic questions and giving silly replies, I needn't go begging help from the neighbors." "You have said more than you know, Sancho," said Don Quixote, "for there are some people who tire themselves out learning and proving things that, once learned and proved, don't matter a straw as far as the mind or memory is concerned." (Cervantes, 1964, p. 682)

Regardless of which interview strategy is used—the informal conversational interview, the interview guide approach, or a standardized open-ended interview—the wording of questions will affect the nature and quality of responses received. Constant attention to the purpose of specific interviews and to the ways in which questions can be worded to achieve that evaluation purpose will reduce the extent to which, in Cervantes's words, evaluators "tire themselves out learning and proving things that, once learned and proved, don't matter a straw as far as the mind or memory is concerned."

The One-Shot Question

Informal, conversational interviewing typically takes place as a natural part of fieldwork. It is opportunistic and often unscheduled. An opportunity presents itself to talk with someone and the interview is underway. More structured and scheduled interviewing takes place as part of formal evaluation site visits. Staff and program participants know that the interview is to take place. Appointments are made and a specific place is set aside for the interview. Yet the best laid plans for scheduled interviews can go awry. The evaluator arrives at the appointed time and place only to find that the person to be interviewed is unwilling to cooperate or needs to run off to take care of some unexpected problem. When faced with such a situation it is helpful to have a single, one-shot question in mind to salvage at least something. This is the question you ask if you are only going to get one shot at the interviewee.

In evaluating an agricultural extension program I was interviewing farmers 150 miles north of the capital city. The farmers in the area were economically distressed and many felt alienated from politicians and professionals. I arrived at a farm for a scheduled interview but the farmer refused to cooperate. At first he refused to even come out of the barn to call off the dogs surrounding my truck. Finally, he appeared and said,

> I don't want to talk to you tonight. I know I said I would, but we've got a family problem and I'm tired and upset. I've always helped with your government surveys. I fill out all the forms the government sends. But I'm tired of it. No more. I don't walk to talk.

I had driven a long way to get this interview. The fieldwork was tightly scheduled, and I knew that I would not get another shot at this farmer, even if he later had a change of heart. To try and salvage the situation, I asked my one-shot question, a question stimulated by his demeanor and overt hostility.

> I'm sorry I caught you at a bad time. But as long as I'm here let me ask you just one quick question. Is there anything you want to tell the bastards in St. Paul?

He hesitated for just a moment and then launched into a tirade that turned into a full, two-hour interview. I never got out of the truck, but I was able to cover the entire interview (though without ever referring to or taking out the written interview schedule). At the end of this conversational interview, which had fully satisfied my data collection needs, he said, "Well, I've enjoyed talkin' with you, and I'm sorry about refusin' to fill out your form. I just don't want to do a survey tonight."

I told him I understood and thanked him for the conversation. My scheduled, structured interview had become an informal, conversational interview developed from a last ditch, one-shot question.

Focus Group Interviews

A focus group interview is an interview with a small group of people on a specific topic. Groups are typically six to eight people who participate in the interview for one-half to two hours.

Focus group interviewing was developed in recognition that many of the consumer decisions that people make are made in a social context, often growing out of discussions with other people. Thus market researchers began using focus groups in the 1950s as a way of simulating the consumer group process of decision making in order to gather more accurate information about consumer product preferences. The classic work on focus group interviews, *The Focused Interview*, was written by Robert K. Merton, Marjorie Fiske, and Patricia L. Kendall in 1956.

The focus group interview is indeed an *interview*. It is not a discussion. It is not a problem-solving session. It is not a decision-making group. It is an *interview*.

The participants are typically a relatively homogeneous group of people who are asked to reflect on the questions asked by the interviewer. Participants get to hear each other's responses and to make additional comments beyond their own original responses as they hear what other people have to say. It is not necessary for the group to reach any kind of consensus. Nor is it necessary for people to disagree. The object is to get high quality data in a social context where people can consider their own views in the context of the views of others.

Focus group interviews have several advantages when used for program evaluation purposes. It is a highly efficient qualitative data collection technique. In one hour the evaluator can gather information from eight people instead of only one person. Thus the sample size can be increased significantly in an evaluation using qualitative methods through focus group interviewing. Focus group interviews also provide some quality controls on data collection in that participants tend to provide checks and balances on each other which weed out false or extreme views. The group dynamics typically contribute to focusing on the most important topics and issues in the program, and it is fairly easy to assess the extent to which there is a relatively consistent, shared view of the program among participants. Finally, focus groups tend to be highly enjoyable to participants.

There are also some weaknesses of focus groups. Since the amount of response time to any given question is increased considerably by having a number of people respond, the number of questions that can be asked is limited. With eight people in an hour, it is typically possible to ask no more than ten major questions. Facilitating and conducting a focus group interview requires considerable group process skill. It is important to know how to manage the interview so that it is not dominated by one or two people, and so that those participants who tend not to be highly verbal are able to share their views.

It can be difficult to take notes during a focus group interview while also facilitating the discussion, so many groups are conducted by pairs of interviewers with one person focusing on taking notes and the other focusing on facilitation. Good notes help in sorting out who said what when the tape recording is transcribed later.

It is always possible that unexpected diversions will occur in a focus group, particularly in an evaluation setting where participants know each other. Conflicts may arise; power struggles may be played out; and status differences may become a factor. In market research, focus groups are typically conducted with people who do not know each other. Of course, when program participants in a focus group do know each other, it is not possible to guarantee confidentiality.

Focus group interviews can be used at any point in the evaluation process. Focus groups can be conducted as part of a needs assessment process with both potential client groups and professionals who know the needs of client groups. Focus groups can be conducted with client groups during a program to identify strengths, weaknesses, and needed improvements. Focus groups can be used at the end of a program, or even months after program completion, to gather perceptions about outcomes and impacts. Key community people can be interviewed in groups when their views of a program may be of interest for evaluation purposes. Focus group interviews can also be used with staff to identify key elements in a program's implementation and treatment. In short, focus groups can be used for a full range of evaluation purposes.

Focus groups are now widely used in market research with quite credible and useful results. This technique is only beginning to be used in evaluation. Focus group interviews, when conducted carefully and used appropriately, promise to provide a rich, new way of gathering qualitative evaluation information.

Recording the Data

The primary data of in-depth, open-ended interviews are quotations. What people say, what they think, how they feel, what they have done, and what they know—these are the things one can learn from talking to people, from interviewing them. The purpose of qualitative interviewing is to understand the perspectives and experiences of the people being interviewed. But no matter what style of interviewing is used, and no matter how carefully one words interview questions, it all comes to naught if the interviewer fails to capture the actual words of the person being interviewed. The raw data of interviews are the actual words spoken by interviewees. There is no substitute for these data.

Tape Recording Interviews

A tape recorder is part of the indispensable equipment of evaluators using qualitative methods. Tape recorders do not tune out of conversations, change what has been said because of interpretation (either conscious or unconscious), or record more slowly than what is being said. (Tape recorders do, however, break down and malfunction.) In addition to increasing the accuracy of data collection, the use of a tape recorder permits the interviewer to be more attentive to the interviewee. The interviewer who is trying to write down everything that is said as it is said will have a difficult time responding appropriately to interviewee needs and cues. The pace of the interview can become decidedly nonconversational. In brief, the interactive nature of in-depth interviewing is seriously affected by the attempt to take verbatim notes during the interview.

This is the major justification for using a tape recorder:

> I'd like to tape record what you have to say so that I don't miss any of it. I don't want to take the chance of relying on my notes and thereby miss something that you say or inadvertently change your words somehow. So, if you don't mind, I'd very much like to use the recorder. If at any time during the interview you would like to turn the tape recorder off, all you have to do is press this button on the microphone, and the recorder will stop.

The use of a tape recorder does not eliminate the need for taking notes. Taking notes can serve at least two purposes: (1) Notes taken during the interview can help the interviewer formulate new questions as the interview moves along, particularly where it may be appropriate to check out something that was said earlier; and (2) taking notes about what is said will facilitate later analysis, including locating important quotations from the tape itself.

The use of a tape recorder does *not* mean that the interviewer can become less attentive to what is being said. This is important regardless

of whether a standardized open-ended interview format is being used or
the more informal, conversational approach.

> One's full attention must be focused on the interview. One must be thinking
> about probing for further explication or clarification of what he is now
> saying; formulating probes; linking up current talk with what he has already
> said; thinking ahead to putting in a *new* question that has now arisen and was
> not taken account of in the standing guide (plus making a note at that
> moment so one will not forget the question); and attending to the interviewee
> in a manner that communicates to him that you are indeed listening. All of
> this is hard enough simply in itself. Add to that the problem of writing it
> down—even if one takes shorthand in an expert fashion—and one can see
> that the process of note-taking in the interview decreases one's interviewing
> capacity. Therefore, if conceivably possible, *tape record;* then one can
> interview. (Lofland, 1971, p. 89)

Transcribing Interviews

Since the raw data of interviews are quotations, the most desirable kind
of data to obtain would be a full transcription of interviews. Although
transcribing is expensive, transcripts can be enormously useful in data
analysis, or later, in replications or independent analyses of the data.

Where resources are not sufficient to permit full transcriptions, the
interviewer can work back and forth between interview notes and
sections of the tape; only those quotations particularly important to the
data analysis and report need be transcribed. In any case, it is critical
that the tape recording be of high quality technically. Few things are
more distressing in collecting qualitative data than to find that the tape
is blank or that background noise is so severe that the tape is virtually
worthless. In the first large-scale interviewing project with which I was
involved, *nearly 20% of the data was lost because of poor quality
recordings.*

Note-Taking During Interviews

When a tape recorder is being used during the interview, notes will
consist primarily of key phrases, lists of major points made by the
respondent, and key terms or words shown in quotation marks that
capture the interviewee's own language. While most interviewers will
not know how to take technical shorthand, it is useful to develop some
system of abbreviations and informal shorthand to facilitate note-
taking. Some important conventions along this line include the

following: (1) Only use quotation marks during note-taking to indicate full and actual quotations; (2) develop some mechanism for indicating interpretations, thoughts, or ideas that occur to you during the interview, for example, the use of brackets to set off your own ideas from those of the interviewee; and (3) keep track of what questions you ask.

When it is not possible to use a tape recorder because of some sensitive situation, interviewee request, or tape recorder malfunction, it is necessary for note-taking to become much more thorough and comprehensive. Again, it is critical to gather actual quotations, as much as possible. This may mean that from time to time, when the interviewee has said something that strikes you as particularly important or insightful, it may be necessary to say, "I'm afraid I need to stop you at this point so that I can get down exactly what you said, because I don't want to lose that particular quotation. Let me read back to you what I have and make sure it is exactly what you said."

With practice and training, an interviewer can learn to use notes for later expansion into more comprehensive detail of what was said in the interview. To do this with accuracy and reliability means reviewing interview notes *immediately following the interview.*

After the Interview

The period after the interview is critical to the rigor and validity of qualitative methods. This is a time for guaranteeing the quality of the data. The first thing to be done after a tape recorded interview is to check the tape to make sure it was recorded properly. If for some reason a malfunction occurred the interviewer should immediately make extensive notes of everything that he or she can remember. Even if the tape functioned properly, the interviewer should go over the interview notes to make certain that what was written makes sense, to identify areas of ambiguity or uncertainty, and to review the quality of information received from the respondent. Did you find out what you really wanted to find out in the interview? If not, what was the problem? Poorly worded questions? Wrong topics? Poor rapport? Do you need to follow up with this person?

It is at this point, immediately following the interview, that observations are written down about the interview itself. *Every good interview is also an observation.* The skilled interviewer listens *and* observes. Nonverbal data are still data. Observational data include where the interview occurred, who was present, how the interviewee reacted to the interview, and any additional information that would help establish a context for interpreting and making sense out of the interview. It is also worth recording observations about yourself as an interviewer. How did your style and approach affect the interview?

This period after the interview is a critical time of reflection and elaboration. *It is a time of quality control to guarantee that the data obtained will be useful, reliable, and valid.* If it is not possible to review the interview immediately afterward, then such a review should occur as soon as practical. Do not rely on your memory. Over time different interviews flow together and who said what becomes muddled.

On occasion this process of immediately reviewing the interview will reveal areas of ambiguity or of uncertainty, where you are not really sure what the person said or meant. As soon as these areas of vagueness turn up the interviewer should check back with the respondent to clarify what was meant. This can often be done over the telephone as a simple way of affirming the accuracy of the interview. In my experience respondents appreciate such follow-up because it indicates the seriousness of the evaluation effort. Guessing at what the person said is absolutely unacceptable. If there is no way of following up the comments with the respondent, then those areas of vagueness and uncertainty simply become missing data.

This period after an interview requires great discipline. Interviewing can be exhausting. It is easy to forego this time of reflection and elaboration, put it off, or neglect it altogether. To do so is to undermine seriously the rigor of qualitative methods. Interviews and observations should be scheduled so that sufficient time is available for data clarification, elaboration, and evaluation.

Examining an interview after it is completed can also be the beginning of analysis. While the situation and data are fresh, insights can occur that might otherwise have been lost. Thus ideas and interpretations that emerge following an interview or observation should be written down and clearly marked as such.

The Personal Side of Interviewing

Interviewing people can be invigorating and stimulating. It is a chance for a short period of time to peer into another person's world. A good interview lays open thoughts, feelings, knowledge, and experiences not only to the interviewer but also to the person answering the questions. The process of being taken through a directed, reflective process affects the person being interviewed. It is not unusual for an interviewee to say, "You know, I hadn't thought of that for a long time." As respondents think about questions they may surprise themselves with fresh insights, previously unarticulated concerns, and new ideas.

I am personally convinced that to be a good interviewer you must like doing it. This means that you are interested in what people have to say. You must yourself believe that the thoughts and experiences of the people being interviewed are worth knowing. In short, you must have the utmost respect for people who are willing to share with you some of their time to help you understand their program experiences and their world.

Researchers have studied the problems that can emerge in attempting to get valid and reliable data from interviewees (e.g., Richardson, Dohrenwend, Snell, & Klein, 1965). Certainly there are uncooperative respondents, people who seem overly sensitive and easily embarrassed, aggressive and hostile interviewees, timid people, and the endlessly verbose who go on at great length about very little. When an interview is going badly it is easy to call forth one of these stereotypes to explain how the interviewee is ruining the interview. Such "blaming of the victim" (the interviewee), however, does little to improve the quality of the data. Nor does it improve interviewing skills.

A different approach is to believe that there is a way to unlock the internal perspectives of every interviewee. It is the task and responsibility of the interviewer to find that interviewing style and that question format which will work with a particular respondent. It is the responsibility of the interviewer to establish an interview climate that facilitates open responses.

When an interview goes well, the interviewer has a right to feel good. When the interview goes badly, it just may be the fault of the person asking the questions. Thus the period of review after an interview can also be a chance to reflect on one's own interviewing skills and to learn from the interviewing experience.

Summary Guidelines for Interviewing

There is no one right way of interviewing, no single correct format that is appropriate for all situations, and no single way of wording questions that will always work. The particular evaluation situation, the needs of the interviewee, and the personal style of the interviewer all come together to create a unique situation for each interview. Therein lie the challenges of depth interviewing: situational responsiveness and sensitivity to get the best data possible.

There is no recipe for effective interviewing, but this chapter has offered some guidelines. These guidelines are summarized below.

(1) Throughout all phases of interviewing, from planning through data collection to analysis, keep centered on the purpose of the evaluation. Let that purpose guide the interviewing process.

(2) The fundamental principle of qualitative interviewing is to provide a framework within which respondents can express their own understandings in their own terms.

(3) Understand the strengths and weaknesses of different types of interviews: the informal conversational interview; the interview guide approach; and the standardized open-ended interview.

(4) Select the type of interview (or combination of types) that is most appropriate to the purposes of the evaluation.

(5) Understand the different kinds of information one can collect through interviews: behavioral data; opinions; feelings; knowledge; sensory data; and background information.

(6) Think about and plan how these different kinds of questions can be most appropriately sequenced for each interview topic, including past, present, and future questions.

(7) Ask truly open-ended questions.

(8) Ask clear questions, using understandable and appropriate language.

(9) Ask one question at a time.

(10) Use probes and follow-up questions to solicit depth and detail.

(11) Communicate clearly what information is desired, why that information is important, and let the interviewee know how the interview is progressing.

(12) Listen attentively and respond appropriately to let the person know he or she is being heard.

(13) Avoid leading questions.

(14) Understand the difference between a depth interview and an interrogation. Qualitative evaluators conduct depth interviews; police investigators and tax auditors conduct interrogations.

(15) Establish personal rapport and a sense of mutual interest.

(16) Maintain neutrality toward the specific content of responses. You are there to collect information not to make judgments about that person.

(17) Observe while interviewing. Be aware of and sensitive to how the person is affected by and responds to different questions.

(18) Maintain control of the interview.

(19) Tape record whenever possible to capture full and exact quotations for analysis and reporting.

(20) Take notes to capture and highlight major points as the interview progresses.

(21) As soon as possible after the interview check the recording for malfunctions; review notes for clarity; elaborate where necessary; and record observations.

(22) Take whatever steps are appropriate and necessary to gather valid and reliable information.

(23) Treat the person being interviewed with respect. Keep in mind that it is a privilege *and* responsibility to peer into another person's experience.

(24) Practice interviewing. Develop your skills.

(25) Enjoy interviewing. Take the time along the way to stop and *hear* the roses.

For Further Reading

Hedges, A. (1985). Group interviewing. In R. Walker (Ed.), *Applied qualitative research.* Brookfield, VT: Gower.

Jones, S. (1985). Depth interviewing. In R. Walker (Ed.), *Applied qualitative research.* Brookfield, VT: Gower.

Lofland, J. (1971). *Analyzing social settings.* Belmont, CA: Wadsworth.

Werner, O., & Schoepfle, M. (1987). *Systematic fieldwork* (Vols. 1-2). Newbury Park, CA: Sage.

Chapter 6
Analyzing and Interpreting
Qualitative Data

The processes of analysis and interpretation involve disciplined study, creative insight, and careful attention to the purposes of the evaluation. Analysis and interpretation are conceptually separate processes. *Analysis* is the process of bringing order to the data, organizing what is there into patterns, categories, and basic descriptive units. *Interpretation* involves attaching meaning and significance to the analysis, explaining descriptive patterns, and looking for relationships and linkages among descriptive dimensions.

There is typically not a precise point at which data collection ends and analysis begins. Nor, in practice, are analysis and interpretation neatly separated. In the course of gathering data, ideas about analysis and interpretation will occur. Those ideas constitute the beginning of analysis. They are part of the record of field notes. Whether one is doing depth interviewing or program observation it is important to keep track of analytic insights that occur during data collection.

The overlapping of data collection and analysis improves both the quality of the data collected and the quality of the analysis so long as the evaluator is careful not to allow initial interpretations to bias additional data collection. Indeed, instead of focusing additional data collection entirely on confirming initial ideas, the evaluator should become particularly sensitive to looking for alternative explanations and contrary patterns that would invalidate initial insights.

When data collection has ended and it is time to begin the formal analysis, the evaluator has two primary sources to draw from in organizing the analysis: (1) the evaluation questions that were generated during the conceptual and design phase of the project and (2) analytic insights and interpretations that emerged during data collection.

Analysis and interpretation take on a specific focus in evaluation.

Evaluation is the systematic collection, analysis, and interpretation of information about the activities and outcomes of actual programs in order for interested persons to make judgments about specific aspects of what the program is doing and improve the program. This general purpose takes its specific focus from the information needs of primary stakeholders and the decision-making context of the particular program being evaluated.

Focusing the Analysis

Focus in analyzing qualitative evaluation data comes from the questions generated at the very beginning of the evaluation process. Many times evaluators go through painstaking care in the process of working with decision makers and stakeholders to conceptualize the evaluation clearly and focus evaluation questions before data collection begins. Then, once the data are collected and analysis begins, they never look back over their notes to renew their understanding of the central issues in the evaluation.

It is not enough to count on remembering what the evaluation questions were. The early negotiations around the purpose of an evaluation usually involve important nuances. To reestablish those nuances for the purpose of helping focus the analysis it is important to review notes on decisions that were made during the conceptual part of the evaluation. This assumes, of course, that the evaluator has treated the conceptual phase of the evaluation as a field experience and has kept detailed notes about the negotiations that went on and the decisions that were made.

It is also appropriate to review the purpose of the evaluation with key decision makers and stakeholders as the formal analysis begins. These discussions will help keep the analysis relevant to the current program situation and will begin preparing the evaluation users for the results. These discussions will often include initial feedback of preliminary findings. Sessions devoted to reestablishing the focus of the evaluation analysis and/or providing initial feedback need to be handled with considerable care. The evaluator will need to explain that the analysis is still preliminary. If, in the course of conducting the more detailed and complete analysis of the data, the evaluator finds that statements made or feedback given during a preliminary session were inaccurate, it is important to let the decision makers and primary stakeholders know about the discrepancy at once.

With a clear sense of the purpose of qualitative evaluation analysis in mind, the evaluator begins the formal data analysis.

Organizing Qualitative Data for Analysis

The data generated by qualitative methods are usually voluminous. I have found no way of preparing students for the sheer mass of information with which they will find themselves confronted when data collection has ended. Sitting down to make sense out of pages of interviews and whole files of field notes can be overwhelming. Just dealing with all those pieces of paper can seem like an impossible task.

The first thing to do is to make sure it is all there. Are the field notes complete? Are there any parts you put off to write later and never got to that need to be finished, even at this late date, before beginning the analysis? Are there any glaring holes that can still be filled by collecting additional data before the analysis begins? Are interview transcriptions complete? Get a sense of the data; check out the quality of the data you have collected.

Once you have reviewed the data, it can be helpful to make at least two complete copies of the main data: one to work on and one original as a basic reference (and for safekeeping). Certain parts of the data will require multiple copies: a copy for writing on, and one or more copies for cutting and pasting. A great deal of the work of qualitative analysis involves creative cutting and pasting of the data. For qualitative analysts able to use microcomputers, much of the organizing and reorganizing of data can be done via word processing. For many, however, the mechanical process of sorting cards, cutting, and pasting will remain the heart of qualitative analysis. It is usually best to have more than one copy for this purpose, for under no circumstances should one yield to the temptation to cut and paste the master copy. The master copy becomes a key resource for locating materials and maintaining the context for the raw data.

The mechanics of organizing data will vary for different people. So will the intellectual process. The analysis of qualitative data is a creative process. There are no formulas, as in statistics. It is a process demanding intellectual rigor and a great deal of hard, thoughtful work. Because different people manage their creativity, intellectual endeavors, and hard work in different ways, there is no one right way to go about organizing, analyzing, and interpreting qualitative data. What follows are suggestions for the basic direction of qualitative analysis rather than rigid rules and procedures.

Qualitative Description

Evaluation reports based on qualitative methods will include a great deal of pure description of the program and the experiences of people in the program. The purpose of this description is to let the reader know what happened in the program, what it was like from the participants' point of view to be in the program, and what particular events or activities in the program were like. In reading through field notes and interviews the evaluator begins to look for those parts of the data that will be polished for presentation as pure description in the evaluation report. What is included by way of description will depend on what questions the evaluation is attempting to answer. Often an entire activity will be reported in detail and depth because it represents a typical program experience. These descriptions are written in narrative form to provide a holistic picture of what has happened in the reported activity or event.

Case Analysis

Cases can be people, groups, critical events, communities, project sites, or subparts of programs. The case is a basic unit of analysis. Chapter 3 discussed different units of analysis and how to sample cases purposefully. When a case approach is used in qualitative analysis, the first step is to pull together the data relevant to each case and write a discrete, holistic case study. Sometimes the entire analysis is only one case. More often there are multiple cases in a qualitative study. After writing the individual case studies, the analysis moves to looking for patterns across cases.

Case data consist of all the information one has about a case, including all the interview data, the observational data, records, impressions and statements of others about the case—in effect, all the information one has accumulated about the particular case in question. These are the raw data for the case analysis. This can amount to a large accumulation of information. At the individual level case data can include clinical records, background information, interviews, observations, life history profiles, and diaries. At the program level case data can include program documents, program reports, interviews with program participants and staff, observations of the program, and program histories.

Writing Case Studies

Once the case data have been accumulated, the first task in case analysis is to write a *case record*. The case record pulls together and organizes the voluminous case data into a comprehensive, primary resource package. The case record includes all the major information that will be used in doing the case analysis and case study. Information is edited, redundancies are sorted out, parts are fitted together, and the case record is organized for ready access either chronologically and/or topically. The case record must be complete but manageable; it should include all the information needed for subsequent analysis, but it is organized at a level beyond that of the raw case data.

> A case record should make no concessions to the reader in terms of interest or communication. It is a condensation of the case data aspiring to the condition that no interpreter requires to appeal behind it to the data to sustain his interpretation. Of course, this criterion cannot be fully met: some case records will be better than others. The case record of a school attempts a portrayal through the organization of data alone, and a portrayal without theoretical aspirations. (Stenhous, 1977, p. 19)

The case record is used to construct a case study. The case study includes the information that will be communicated in the final report; it represents the data presentation in the report. The report may consist of several case studies which are then compared and contrasted, but the basic data of the study is the information provided about the cases. The case study is the descriptive, analytic, interpretive, and evaluative treatment of the more comprehensive descriptive data that are in the case record. Table 6.1 shows this sequence in moving from raw case data to the written case study.

The case study should take the reader into the case situation—a person's life, a group's life, or a program's life. Each case study in a report stands alone, allowing the reader to understand the case holistically. At a later point in analysis it is possible to compare and contrast cases, but initially each case must be represented and understood as an idiosyncratic and unique phenomenon. The descriptions of the cases should be holistic and comprehensive, given the focus of evaluation, and will include myriad dimensions, factors, variables, and categories woven together into an ideographic framework.

How one compares and contrasts cases will depend on the purpose of the evaluation. The way in which cases were sampled will have an important bearing on how case studies are used in analysis. Critical cases, extreme cases, typical cases, and varied cases serve different evaluation purposes.

Once case studies have been organized and written the analytic strategies described in the remainder of this chapter can be used to further analyze and interpret the case study data.

TABLE 6.1
The Process of Constructing Case Studies

Step 1:   *Assemble the raw case data.*

These data consist of all the information collected about the person or program for which a case study is to be written.

Step 2:   *Construct a case record.*

This is a condensation of the raw case data organizing, classifying, and editing the raw case data into a manageable and accessible package.

Step 3:   *Write a case study narrative.*

The case study is a readable, descriptive picture of a person or program that makes accessible to the reader all the information necessary to understand that person or program. The case study is presented either chronologically or thematically (sometimes both). The case study presents a holistic portrayal of a person or program.

Content Analysis

Content analysis involves identifying coherent and important examples, themes, and patterns in the data. The analyst looks for quotations or observations that go together, that are examples of the same underlying idea, issue, or concept. Sometimes this involves pulling together all the data that address a particular evaluation question. For example, a question in a process evaluation might concern the nature of staff interactions with program participants. The evaluation analyst first pulls together all the data related to this issue, then subdivides that data into coherent categories, patterns, and themes.

The evaluator typically begins by reading through field notes, interviews, and case studies while writing comments in the margins indicating what can be done with the different parts of the data. This is the beginning of organizing the data into topics and files. Coming up with topics is like constructing an index for a book or labels for a file system; you look at what is there and give it a name, a label. The copy on which these topics and labels are written becomes the indexed copy of your field notes, interviews, or case studies. Several readings of the data are usually necessary before it can be completely indexed.

Labeling the data and establishing a data index are first steps in content analysis. The contents of the data are being classified. A classification system is critical; without classification there is chaos.

Organizing and simplifying the complexity of data into some meaningful and manageable themes or categories is the basic purpose of content analysis.

Where more than one person is working on the analysis, or where an evaluator has assistance in conducting the analysis, it is helpful to have more than one person classify the data. Each person content analyzes the data separately and then the results are compared and discussed. Important insights can emerge from the different ways in which two people look at the same set of data.

Inductive Analysis

Inductive analysis means that the patterns, themes, and categories of analysis come from the data; they emerge out of the data rather than being decided prior to data collection and analysis. The analyst looks for natural variation in the data. For evaluators, the study of natural variation will involve particular attention to variations in program processes and the ways in which participants respond to and are affected by programs.

Two kinds of patterns may emerge from analysis of the data. First, the analyst can use the categories developed and articulated by people in the program studied to organize presentation of particular themes. Second, the analyst may also become aware of categories or patterns for which the people in the program did not have labels or terms, and the analyst then develops terms to describe these inductively generated categories. Each of these approaches to analysis is described below.

Indigenous Typologies

Typologies are classification systems made up of categories that divide some aspect of the world into parts. Indigenous typologies have in anthropology come to be called the "emic" approach to analysis.

> According to this view, cultural behavior should always be studied and categorized in terms of the inside view—the actors' definition—of human events. That is, the units of conceptualization in anthropological theories should be 'discovered' by analyzing the cognitive processes of the people studied, rather than 'imposed' from cross-cultural (hence, ethnocentric) classifications of behavior. (Pelto & Pelto, 1978, p. 54)

This kind of approach requires an analysis of the verbal categories used by participants and/or staff in a program to break up the complexity of reality into parts. It is a fundamental purpose of language to tell us what is important by giving it a name and therefore separating it from other things with other names. Once these labels have been identified from an analysis of what people in the program have said, the next step is to identify the attributes or characteristics that distinguish one thing from another. In describing this kind of analysis Charles Frake (1962) uses the example of a hamburger. Hamburgers can vary a great deal; there are many ways to prepare them or add to them, and yet they are still called hamburgers. However, when a piece of cheese is added to the meat, it is no longer a hamburger; it becomes a cheeseburger. The task for the analyst is to discover what separates "hamburger" from "cheeseburger." The purpose of this analysis is to discern and report "how people construe their world of experience from the way they talk about it" (Frake, 1962, p. 74).

An evaluation example of this kind of analysis comes from work we did in evaluating a program aimed at reducing the dropout rate among high school students. In observations and interviews at the targeted high school it became important to understand the ways in which teachers categorized students. With regard to problems of truancy, absenteeism, tardiness, and skipping class, the teachers had come to label students as either "chronics" or "borderlines." One teacher described the chronics as "the ones who are out there all the time and everything you do to get them in doesn't work." Another teacher said, "you can always pick them out, the chronics. They're usually the same kids." The borderlines, on the other hand, "skip a few classes, waiting for a response, and when it comes they shape up. They're not so different from your typical junior high student, but when they see the chronics getting away with it they get more brazen in their actions." Another teacher said, "Borderlines are the ones who act up maybe two and three times a day, not constantly like the chronics."

Not all teachers used precisely the same criteria to distinguish "chronics" from "borderlines," but all teachers used these labels in talking about students. One of the tasks of qualitative analysis was to portray and understand the teachers' views about dropouts as represented by this indigenous typology.

It became clear that in understanding the impact of the program on students, and the nature of program activities directed at reducing high school dropouts, it would be important to observe differences in the program between borderlines and chronics. It was difficult to get the teachers, in many cases, to even attempt to deal with the chronics.

It would have been impossible to understand fully the situations in that program as conceived by the teachers and experienced by the students without understanding this indigenous typology of "chronics" and "borderlines." Moreover, this typology had important implications for how the program was organized and the extent to which different strategies were to be developed to deal with different kinds of students. These categories, then, became themes which were important throughout the data analysis and the final report.

Every program gives rise to a special vocabulary which staff and participants can use to differentiate types of activities, different kinds of participants, different styles of participation, and different contributions to the program. These indigenous typologies are clues to the evaluator that the phenomena to which the labels refer are important to the people in the setting, and that to fully understand the setting it is necessary to understand those terms and their implications for the program.

Analyst-Constructed Typologies

While program staff and participants will have developed typologies for certain important features of the program, other important patterns may not have given rise to specific linguistic distinctions within the program. The second task of induction, then, is for the analyst to look for patterns, categories, and themes that appear to exist but that are not a part of participants' vocabulary. A typology can then be constructed to elucidate variations and contrasts in activities, participants, and/or staff. One major way of finding out whether or not such analyst-constructed typologies are accurate and useful is to present them to people in the program to find out if the constructions make sense.

A good example of this kind of evaluator-generated typology is to be found in the evaluation of the National Museum of Natural History, Smithsonian Institution, directed by Robert L. Wolf and Barbara L. Tymitz (1977). They conducted a naturalistic inquiry of the "Ice Age Mammals and Emergence of Man" exhibit at the museum. From their observations, they identified four different kinds of visitors to the exhibit.

The Commuter

This is the person who merely uses the hall as a vehicle to get from the entry point to the exit point. . . .

The Nomad

This is a casual visitor—a person who is wandering through the hall, apparently open to become interested in *something*. The Nomad is not really sure why he or she is in the hall and not really sure that s/he is going to find anything interesting in this particular exhibit hall. Occasionally the Nomad stops, but it does not appear that the nomadic visitor finds any one thing in the hall more interesting than any other thing.

The Cafeteria Type

This is the interested visitor who *wants* to get interested in something, and so the entire museum and the hall itself is treated as a cafeteria. Thus, the person walks along, hoping to find something of interest, hoping to "put something on his or her tray" and stopping from time to time in the hall. While it appears that there is something in the hall that spontaneously sparks the person's interest, we perceive this visitor has a predilection to becoming interested, and the exhibit provides the many things from which to choose.

The V.I.P.—Very Interested Person

This visitor comes into the hall with some prior interest in the content area. This person may not have come specifically to the hall, but once there, the hall serves to remind the V.I.P's that they were, in fact, interested in something in that hall beforehand. The V.I.P. goes through the hall much more carefully, much slower, much more critically—that is, they move from point to point, they stop, they examine aspects of the hall with a greater degree of scrutiny and care. (Wolf & Tymitz, 1977, pp. 10-11)

This typology of visitors became important in the full evaluation because it permitted analysis of different kinds of museum experiences and different activities undertaken in the museum. Moreover, the authors recommended that when conducting interviews with museum visitors to get their reactions to exhibits that the interview data be differentially valued depending on the type of person who was being interviewed.

The primary purpose of typologies is to *describe* and *classify*. These typologies can later be used to make interpretations about the nature of the program, but the first purpose is description based on an analysis of the patterns that appear in the data. But how does one recognize patterns in qualitative data and turn those patterns into meaningful categories?

Developing Category Systems

Guba (1978) suggests that in focusing the analysis of qualitative data an evaluator must deal first with the problem of "convergence." The problem of convergence is figuring out what things fit together. This leads to a classification system for the data.

Guba suggests several steps for converging field notes and observations about issues and concerns into systematic categories of analysis. The evaluator-analyst begins by looking for "recurring regularities" in the data. These regularities represent patterns that can be sorted into categories. Categories should then be judged by two criteria: "internal homogeneity" and "external heterogeneity." The first criterion concerns the extent to which the data that belong in a certain category hold together or "dovetail" in a meaningful way." The second criterion concerns the extent to which differences among categories are bold and clear. "The existence of a large number of unassignable or overlapping data items is good evidence of some basic fault in the category system" (Guba, 1978, p. 53). The naturalistic evaluator then works back and forth between the data and the classification system to verify the meaningfulness and accuracy of the categories and the placement of data in categories.

The second problem discussed by Guba is the problem of "divergence." By this he means that the evaluator must deal with how to "flesh out" the categories. He suggests that this is done by processes of extension (building on items of information already known), bridging (making connections among different items), and surfacing (proposing new information that ought to fit and then verifying its existence). The analyst brings closure to the process when sources of information have been exhausted, when sets of categories have been saturated so that new sources lead to redundancy, when clear regularities have emerged that feel integrated, and when the analysis begins to "overextend" beyond the boundaries of the issues and concerns guiding the analysis.

The steps and procedures suggested by Guba for analyzing qualitative data are not mechanical or rigid. The process of data analysis is to a major extent "arty" and "intuitive."

This effort at uncovering patterns, themes, and categories is a creative process that requires making carefully considered judgments about what is really significant and meaningful in the data. Since qualitative analysts do not have statistical tests to tell them when an observation or pattern is significant, they must rely on their own intelligence, experience, and judgment.

Logical Analysis

While working inductively the analyst is looking for emergent patterns in the data. These patterns, as noted in the preceding sections, can be represented as dimensions, classification schemes, and categories. Once some dimensions have been constructed, either using participant-generated constructions or evaluator-generated constructions, it is sometimes useful to cross-classify different dimensions to generate new insights about how the data can be organized and to look for patterns that may not have been immediately obvious in the initial, inductive analysis. Creating cross-classification matrices is an exercise in logic. This procedure involves creating potential categories by crossing one dimension or typology with another, and then working back and forth between the data and one's logical constructions, filling in the resulting matrix. This logical system will create a new typology, all parts of which may or may not actually be represented by the data. Thus the analyst moves back and forth between the logical construction and the actual data in the ongoing search for understanding through description. The analysis presented in the next section shows how a matrix can be created by cross-classifying program processes and program outcomes to organize the linkages between processes and outcomes in qualitative analysis.

A Process/Outcomes Matrix

The linkage between processes and outcomes is a fundamental issue in many program evaluations. In Chapter 2, I suggested that a qualitative evaluation design might be particularly appropriate where either program processes or program impacts, or both, were largely unspecified, for whatever reasons. Sometimes the reason is because outcomes were meant to be individualized; sometimes the program is simply uncertain about what the outcomes will be; and in many programs neither processes nor impacts have been carefully articulated. Under such conditions one purpose of the evaluation may be to help articulate program processes, program impacts, and the linkages between the two. This task can be facilitated by constructing a process/outcomes matrix to organize the data.

Figure 6.1 is an abstraction of how such a matrix can be constructed. Major program processes or identified implementation components are listed along the left side. Types or levels of outcomes are listed across the top. The category systems for program processes and outcomes are developed from the data in the same way that other typologies are constructed (see previous sections). The cross-classification of any process with any outcome produces a cell in the matrix; for example, the first cell in Figure 6.1 is created by the intersection of process 1 with outcome a. The information that goes in cell 1-a (or any other cell in the matrix) describes linkages, patterns, themes, program content, or actual activities that help us understand the relationships between processes and outcomes. Such relationships may have been identified by participants themselves during interviews or discovered by the evaluator in analyzing the data. In either case, the process/outcomes matrix becomes a way of organizing, thinking about, and presenting the qualitative connections between program implementation dimensions and program impacts.

An example may help make the notion of the process-outcomes matrix more concrete. Suppose we have been evaluating a juvenile justice program which places delinquent youths in foster homes. We have visited several foster homes; observed what the home environments are like; and interviewed the juveniles, the foster home parents, and the probation officers. A regularly recurring theme in the interviews is the importance of the process of "letting kids learn to make their own decisions." A regularly recurring outcomes theme is "keeping the kids straight" (reduce recidivism). The blank cell in a matrix created by crossing the program process ("kids making their own decisions") with the program outcome ("keeping kids straight") creates a data analysis question: What actual decisions do juveniles make that are supposed to lead to reduced recidivism? We then carefully review our field notes and interview quotations looking for data that help us understand how people in the progam have answered this question based on their actual behaviors and practices. By describing what decisions juveniles actually make in the program the decision makers to whom our findings are reported can make their own judgments about the strength or weakness of this linkage between this program process and the desired outcome. Moreover, once the descriptive analysis is complete the evaluator is at liberty to offer interpretations and judgments about the nature and quality of this supposed process/outcome connection.

Causes, Consequences, and Relationships

Thus far the data analysis has emphasized the tasks of organization and description. Even the process/outcomes matrix was aimed at providing a mechanism for organizing and describing the themes, patterns, activities, and content of the program, rather than at elucidating causal linkages between processes and outcomes. As the process/outcomes

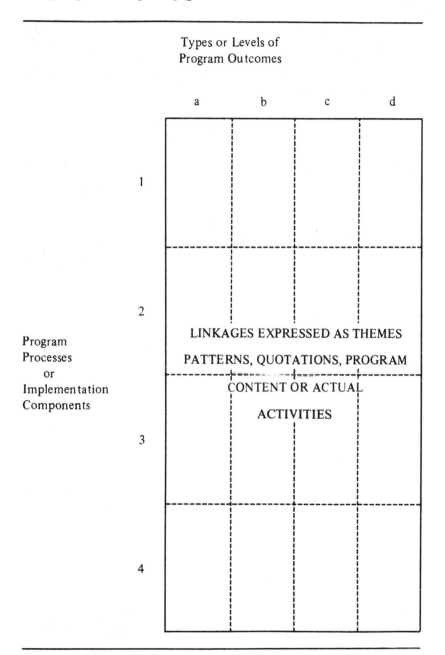

Figure 6.1 Matrix of linkages between program processes and impacts.

matrix demonstrates, however, there is often a fine line between description and causal interpretation. To the extent that one is *describing* the causal linkages suggested by and believed in by program participants and staff, the evaluator-analyst has not crossed the line from description into causal interpretation. Once the tasks of organization and description are complete it may then be appropriate to move on to considerations of causes, consequences, and relationships.

Naturalistic inquiry is not aimed at testing causal propositions. Thus interpretations about which things appear to lead to other things, which parts of the setting produce certain effects, and how processes lead to outcomes are necessarily areas of evaluator speculation, conjecture, and hypothesizing. Yet when careful study of the data gives rise to ideas about causal linkages, there is no reason to deny decision makers and stakeholders the benefit of those insights simply because they cannot be "proven." It is important that such statements be clearly qualified as what they are—speculation and conjecture, but *data-based speculation and conjecture.* The evaluator who has studied the program, lived with the data from the field, and reflected at length about the patterns and themes that run through the data can reasonably be expected to speculate, make conjectures, and formulate hypotheses. If decision makers and information users are interested in these kinds of interpretations, there is no reason not to share insights to help them think about their own causal presuppositions, ideas, and theories.

Such conjectures or speculations should not, however, be derived simply from the theoretical predispositions of the evaluator. *The cardinal principle of qualitative analysis is that causal and theoretical statements be clearly emergent from and grounded in field observations. The theory emerges from the data; it is not imposed on the data.*

One of the greatest difficulties for evaluators engaged in qualitative analysis is that when they begin to consider causes, consequences, and interdependent relationships they fall back on the linear assumptions of quantitative analysis and begin to specify isolated variables that are mechanically linked together out of context. In attempting to present a holistic picture of what the program is like and in struggling to understand the phenomenological nature of a particular set of activities and people in a specific context, simple statements of linear relationships may be more distorting than illuminating. It is the ongoing challenge of qualitative analysis that we maintain perspective as we move back and forth between the real world of the program and our abstractions of that program, between the descriptions of what has occurred and our analysis of those descriptions, between the complexity of reality and our simplifications of that complexity, between the circularities and inter-dependencies of human activity and our desire for linear, ordered statements of cause and effect.

Validation and Verification

Preceding sections have presented strategies for organizing and making sense of qualitative data. The remainder of this chapter will be concerned with the problem of deciding how much to trust the data analysis. There are two aspects to the issue of trusting the data. First, the evaluators analyzing the data must determine how much confidence to place in their own analysis. Second, the data analysis must be presented to stakeholders in such a way that they can verify and validate the findings for themselves. There are several major strategies for validating and verifying the results of qualitative analysis.

Rival Explanations

Once the evaluator has described and interpreted major patterns, themes, and linkages that have emerged from the analysis, it is important to look for rival or competing themes and explanations. This can be done both inductively and logically. Inductively, the search for rival explanations involves looking for other ways of organizing the data that might lead to different findings. Logically, rival explanations come from thinking about other logical possibilities and then seeing if those possibilities can be supported by the data.

When considering rival hypotheses and competing explanations the analyst does not attempt to disprove these alternatives. Rather, the analyst looks for data that *support* alternative explanations. This is a matter of intellectual integrity. Failure to find strong supporting evidence for alternative explanations helps increase confidence in the original, principal explanation generated by the analyst. It is unlikely that comparing alternative explanations or looking for data in support of alternative patterns will lead to clear-cut "yes there is support" versus "no there is no support" kinds of conclusions. It is a matter of considering the *weight* of evidence and looking for the *best* fit between data and analysis. It is important to report whatever alternative explanations are considered and "tested" during data analysis. Reporting on what rival explanations were considered, and how those alternatives were considered, lends credibility to the final set of findings reported by the evaluator.

Negative Cases

Closely related to the testing of rival explanations is the search for negative cases. Our understanding of qualitative patterns is increased by considering the instances and cases that do not fit the pattern. These are the "exceptions that prove the rule," or for evaluation purposes, cases that elucidate the findings. Examples that do not fit help clarify the limits and meaning of the primary pattern.

The evaluator must be as intellectually honest in attempting to support alternative hypotheses and to understand negative or deviant cases as he or she was in building support from the data for the original explanation. The users of the evaluation findings will then be able to make their own decisions about the plausibility of alternate explanations and the reasons that deviant cases do not fit within dominant patterns.

What is discovered during analysis must be verified by going back to the data under study and examining the extent to which the emergent analysis really fits the program and works to explain what has been observed. Glaser and Strauss describe what it means for results to fit and work. "By 'fit' we mean that the categories must be readily (not forcibly) applicable to and indicated by the data under study; by 'work' we mean that they must be meaningfully relevant to and be able to explain the behavior under study" (Glaser & Strauss, 1967, p. 3). Discovery and verification mean moving back and forth between induction and deduction, between experience and reflection on experience.

The section of the evaluation report that explores rival explanations and cases that do not quite fit the dominant pattern can be among the most interesting sections of a report. When well-written this section of a report reads something like a detective novel where the detective (evaluator) is looking for clues that lead in different directions and trying to sort out which direction makes the most sense given the clues (data) that are available. Moreover, the whole tone of a report is quite different when the evaluator is willing to consider openly other possibilities than those finally presented as most reasonable. Compare the approach of weighing alternatives to one where all the data lead in a single-minded fashion toward an overwhelming presentation of a single point of view. Which is more interesting? Which is more credible?

Triangulation to Strengthen Analysis

Chapter 3 on design discussed the importance of using different data collection techniques and different research strategies to study the same program. It is in data analysis that this strategy of triangulation really pays off. Four types of triangulation were discussed in Chapter 3: (1) collecting different kinds of data on the same question; (2) using different fieldworkers and interviewers to avoid the biases of any one person working alone; (3) using multiple methods to study a program; and (4) using different perspectives (or theories) to interpret a set of data.

Triangulation is seldom a straightforward process in analysis. For example, it can turn out that quantitative methods and qualitative methods will end up answering different questions that do not easily come together to provide a single, well-integrated picture of the situation. Shapiro (1973) has described at length her struggle to resolve basic differences between qualitative and quantitative data in her study of elementary school classrooms. She eventually concluded that some of the conflicts between the two kinds of data were a result of measuring quite different things although the ways in which different things were measured were not immediately apparent until she worked to sort out the conflicting findings. She began with greater trust in the data derived from quantitative methods and ended up believing that the most useful information came from the qualitative data. The point for our purposes is that what she hoped would be mutually reinforcing methods and data ended up being quite conflicting. Resolving the conflicts, however, greatly enriched the ultimate analysis.

Similar difficulties can emerge from qualitative methods where the evaluator has triangulated qualitative data sources. This means comparing observational data with interview data; it means comparing what people say in public with what they say in private; it means checking the consistency of what people say over time; and it means comparing the perspectives of people with different points of view. It means validating information obtained through interviews by checking program documents and other written evidence that can corroborate what interview respondents report. Sometimes these divergent types of data provide a consistent picture. At other times the different data sources point in different directions. It is best not to expect everything to turn out the same. The point is to study and understand when and why there are differences. Finding that observational data produce different results than interview data does not mean that either or both kinds of data are invalid. More likely, it means that different kinds of data have captured different things, so the analyst attempts to understand the reasons for the differences. At the same time, consistency in overall patterns of data from different sources and reasonable explanations for differences in data from various sources contribute significantly to the overall credibility of the findings presented in the evaluation report.

Keeping Methods and Data in Context

One possible source of distortion in findings of qualitative evaluation reports is the nature of research design decisions used for data collection. Thus it is important to consider the rival methodological hypothesis that the findings are due to distortions introduced by the sampling strategies used in the study. Three kinds of sampling errors can arise in qualitative research designs: There may be distortion in the situations that were sampled for observation (since it is seldom possible to observe all situations); there may be distortions introduced by the time periods during which observations took place—that is, problems of temporal sampling; and third, the findings may be distorted because of selectivity in the people who were sampled either for observations or interviews. In considering how sampling strategies may have affected evaluation findings, the analyst returns to consideration of the reasons for having made initial design decisions (see Chapter 3). To the extent that those design decisions were based directly on the kinds of evaluation questions that were being asked, apparent distortions produced by sampling decisions may have been purposeful and deliberate given a calculated desire to study intensively only certain situations, certain time periods, or certain people. Under these conditions the problem is no longer one of distortion of the data actually collected, but is a question of the extent to which the findings can be generalized to other situations, other time periods, and other people. Thus the evaluator-analyst must be careful to limit conclusions to those situations, time periods, persons, and contexts for which the data are applicable.

The importance of reporting both methods selected and resulting data in their proper contexts cannot be overemphasized. *Keeping things in context is a cardinal principle of qualitative analysis.*

Reporting Findings

The actual content and format of a qualitative evaluation report will depend on the information needs of primary stakeholders and the purpose of the evaluation. Even a comprehensive report will have to omit a great deal of the data collected by the evaluator. Focus is essential. Analysts who try to include everything risk losing their readers in the sheer volume of the presentation. Lofland (1971, p. 123) calls the decisions that must be made about what material to leave out of a report "the agony of omitting." The agony of omitting on the part of the researcher is matched only by the readers' agony in having to read those things that were not omitted—but should have been.

Balance Between Description and Analysis

In considering what to omit, a decision has to be made about how much description to include. Detailed description and in-depth quotations are the essential qualities of qualitative reports. Sufficient description and direct quotations should be included to allow readers to understand fully the program and the thoughts of the people represented in the report. Description should stop short, however, of becoming trivial and mundane. The reader does not have to know absolutely everything that was done or said. Again the problem of focus arises.

Description is balanced by analysis and interpretation. Endless description becomes its own muddle. The purpose of analysis is to organize the description in a way that makes it manageable. Description is balanced by analysis and leads into interpretation. An interesting and readable report provides sufficient description to allow the reader to understand the analysis and sufficient analysis to allow the reader to understand the interpretations and explanations presented.

Verification and validation information are added wherever relevant. Remarks throughout the text about the nature and extent of triangulation, validity checks, and supporting evidence are helpful to the reader as findings are presented.

It is also important that the analyst *not* pretend that all findings are equally credible. The evaluator bears some responsibility to help stakeholders and other readers of the report sort out the strengths and weaknesses of various parts of the description and analysis. Qualitative analysis does not have the parsimonious statistical significance tests of quantitative analysis. Statistical tests of significance are shorthand ways of telling the reader how seriously to take quantitative findings. In qualitative reports the analyst must make substantive judgments about variations in the credibility of different findings. When are patterns "clear," when are they "strongly supported by the data," and when are the patterns "weak"? Substantive significance is a matter of judgment.

Readers will end up making their own decisions and judgments about these matters, but the evaluator's opinions and perspective deserve to be reported. No one knows the data better than the analyst who has struggled to make sense out of findings and then tried to communicate that sense in a report. Thus, as in all other aspects of qualitative methods, the person conducting the inquiry is the critical element in determining validity, meaningfulness of the findings, and credibility.

For Further Reading

Fetterman, D. M. (Ed.). (1984). *Ethnography in educational evaluation.* Newbury Park, CA: Sage.

Fielding, N., & Fielding, J. (1986). *Linking data.* Newbury Park, CA: Sage.

Glaser, B. G., & Strauss, A. L. (1967). *Discovery of grounded theory: Strategies for qualitative research.* Chicago: AVC.

Guba, E. G. (1978). *Toward a methodology of naturalistic inquiry in educational evaluation* (CSE Mongraph Series in Evaluation No. 8). Los Angeles: Center for the Study of Evaluation.

Lofland, J. (1971). *Analyzing social settings.* Belmont, CA: Wadsworth.

Miles, M., & Huberman, M. (1984). *Qualitative data analysis.* Newbury Park, CA: Sage.

Patton, M. Q. (1980a). Making methods choices. *Evaluation and program planning, 3,* 219-228.

Patton, M. Q. (1980b). *Qualitative evaluation methods.* Newbury Park, CA: Sage.

Chapter 7
Making Methods Decisions:
Controversy and Philosophy

This final chapter is meant to place decisions about using qualitative methods within a larger philosophical context. The use of qualitative methods can be quite controversial. The controversy stems from a longstanding debate in science over how best to study and understand the world. The debate is rooted in philosophical differences about the nature of reality.

It is not possible to review these issues fully here. Other sources provide a detailed discussion of what has come to be called "the paradigms debate," a paradigm being a particular world view (see Cronbach, 1975; Guba & Lincoln, 1981; Patton, 1986; Reichardt & Cook, 1979). The point here is to alert evaluators to the intensity of the debate. It is important to be aware that both scientists and nonscientists often hold strong opinions about what constitutes credible evidence and that the dominant view often has favored quantitative data. Given the potentially controversial nature of methods decisions, evaluators interested in using qualitative methods need to be prepared to explain and defend the value and appropriateness of qualitative approaches. This chapter will briefly provide responses to the most common concerns.

Beyond the Numbers Game

How can one deal with a bias against qualitative methods? The starting point is understanding and being able to communicate the particular strengths of qualitative methods and the kinds of evaluation questions for which qualitative data are especially appropriate. These were the subjects of Chapters 1 and 2 in this book.

It is also helpful to understand the special seductiveness of numbers in modern society. Numbers convey a sense of precision and accuracy even if the measurements which yielded the numbers are relatively unreliable, invalid, and meaningless. The point, however, is not to be anti-numbers. The point is to be pro-meaningfulness. Thus by knowing the strengths and weaknesses of both quantitative and qualitative data, the evaluator can help stakeholders focus on really important questions rather than, as sometimes happens, focusing primarily on how to generate numbers. The really important questions are: What is worth knowing about the program? What data will be most useful? How can the design be appropriately matched to the evaluation situation, the stage of program development, and the primary information needs of stakeholders?

Concerns About Objectivity and Truth

Perhaps the most common concern about qualitative methods is the subjectivity of the evaluator. Science places great value on objectivity. Often the primary reason decision makers commission an evaluation is to get objective data from an objective scientist.

A parallel concern is getting at the truth. A search for TRUTH suggests a single right answer. Qualitative methods, however, assume mutiple perspectives and multiple "truths" depending on different points of view. How, then, does one respond to concerns about objectivity and truth?

It is helpful to know that philosophers of science now typically doubt the possibility of anyone or any method being really "objective." Philosopher and evaluator Michael Scriven (1972b) has further argued, quite persuasively, that quantitative methods are no more synonymous with objectivity than qualitative methods are synonymous with subjectivity. The ways in which tests and questionnaires are constructed are no less open to the intrusion of evaluator's biases than the making of observations in the field or the asking of questions in interviews. Numbers do not protect against bias; they sometimes merely disguise it. All statistical data are based on *someone's* definition of what to measure and how to measure it. An "objective" statistic, such as the consumer price index, is really made up of very subjective decisions about what consumer items to include in the index. Periodically government economists change the basis and definition of such indices.

Guba (1978) has considered the issues of objectivity and subjectivity with special reference to evaluation. He notes that all kinds of evaluation data should be reliable, factual, and confirmable. "There seems to be no intrinsic reason why the methods of a properly trained naturalistic inquirer should be any more doubtful a source of such data than the methods of an investigator using a more quantitative approach" (Guba, 1978, pp. 74-75). He and others (e.g., House, 1980) have suggested that the issue is more clearly stated as the "neutrality" of the evaluator rather than objectivity or subjectivity. The neutral evaluator is impartial, one who is not predisposed toward certain findings ahead of time. The neutral evaluator enters the field with no axe to grind, no theory to prove, and no predetermined results to support.

In short, then, concerns about objectivity can often be better understood and discussed as concerns about neutrality. The possibility of attaining objectivity and truth in any absolute sense has become an untenable position in evaluation. Yet the negative connotations associated with the term "subjectivity" make it an unacceptable alternative. The practical solution may be to replace the traditional search for truth with a search for useful and balanced information, and to replace the mandate to be objective with a mandate to be fair and conscientious in taking account of multiple perspectives, multiple interests, and multiple possibilities.

Concerns About Generalizing

Another common concern about qualitative methods is the small sample size usually involved and the impossibility of generalizing. Chapter 3 discussed the logic and value of purposeful sampling with few, but carefully selected, information-rich cases. However, purposeful sampling is not widely understood. Thus evaluators can often expect to encounter a predisposition toward large and random samples.

It is important in responding to such concerns that one fully understand the relative strengths and weaknesses of different sampling strategies. And qualitative and quantitative samples are not incompatible. The design chapter discusses several mutually reinforcing combinations.

Still, there are deeper philosophical issues involved in concerns about generalizing. Part of the problem is distinguishing program evaluation from more basic scientific investigations. While scientists search for universal laws and generalizations across time and space, evaluators tend to focus on providing useful information that is fairly specific to one or a few programs.

Moreover, qualitative evaluators tend to be philosophically and methodologically skeptical of generalizations based on statistical inferences drawn from data collected at one or a few points in a program's life. Findings based on samples, however large, are often stripped of their context when generalizations are made—particularly generalizations across time and space. Cronbach (1975) has observed that generalizations decay over time—that is, they have a half-life as do radioactive materials. Guba and Lincoln (1981) ask, "What can a generalization be except an assertion that is context free? . . . [Yet] *it is virtually impossible to imagine any human behavior that is not heavily mediated by the context in which it occurs*" (p. 62).

Cronbach (1980) has offered a middle ground in the methodological paradigms debate over generalizability and the relevance of evaluations. He argues against experimental designs that are so focused on carefully controlling cause and effect that the findings are largely irrelevant beyond that highly controlled experimental situation. On the other hand, he is equally concerned that entirely idiosyncratic case studies may yield little that is useful beyond the case study setting. He is doubtful that highly specific generalizations will hold up across time and space. He suggests instead that designs balance depth and breadth, realism and control so as to permit reasonable "extrapolation" (pp. 231-235).

Unlike the usual meaning of the term "generalization," an extrapolation clearly connotes that one has gone beyond the narrow confines of the data to think about other applications of the findings. Extrapolations are modest speculations on the likely applicability of findings to other situations under similar, but not identical, conditions. Extrapolations are logical, thoughtful, and problem-oriented rather than statistical and probabilistic. Extrapolations can be particularly useful when based on information-rich samples and designs (i.e., on evaluations which produce relevant information carefully targeted to stakeholder concerns about both the present and the future). Users of evaluation will usually expect evaluators to extrapolate thoughtfully from their findings in the sense of pointing out lessons learned and potential applications to future efforts. Sampling strategies in qualitative evaluations can be planned with the stakeholders' desire for extrapolation in mind.

The Increased Legitimacy of
Qualitative Methods in Evaluation

In the early literature on evaluation methods the debate between qualitative and quantitative methodologies was often strident. In recent years the debate has softened. A consensus has gradually emerged that the important challenge is to match appropriate methods to evaluation questions and issues, not to advocate universally any single methodological approach for all evaluation situations.

The increased legitimacy of qualitative evaluation methods is also a function of more and higher quality training; the publication of a substantial qualitative evaluation literature; more examples of useful, high-quality evaluations employing qualitative methods; and an increased commitment to providing useful and understandable information based on stakeholders' concerns. In short, evaluation has moved into a period of methodological diversity with a focus on methodological appropriateness.

Selecting Appropriate Evaluation Methods

Selecting appropriate evaluation methods is no easy task. Today's evaluators must be sophisticated about matching research methods to the nuances of particular evaluation questions, the idiosyncrasies of specific program situations, and the information needs of identifiable stakeholders.

This means that evaluators must have a large repertoire of research methods and techniques available to use on a variety of problems. Thus today's evaluator may be called on to use any and all social science research methods, including survey research techniques, social indicators, cost-benefit analysis, standardized tests, experimental or quasi-experimental designs, unobtrusive measures, participant observation, and depth interviewing.

The skilled evaluator works to design a study that includes any and all data that will help shed light on the evaluation questions being investigated, given constraints of limited resources and time. The evaluator is committed to designs that are relevant, rigorous, understandable, and able to produce useful results that are valid, reliable, and believable. On many occasions and for many situations a variety of data collection techniques and design approaches will be desirable. Multiple methods and triangulation of observations can contribute to methodological rigor.

Of course, the ideal of the evaluator being methodologically flexible, sophisticated, and able to use a variety of methods to study any particular evaluation question runs headlong into the realities of limited resources, political considerations, and the narrow disciplinary training available to most evaluators. These constraints mean that the imagery of being skilled and sophisticated includes the evaluator as negotiator, striving to obtain the best possible design and the most useful answers within the real world of politics, people, and methodological imperfections.

Attempting to select appropriate research methods is clearly a difficult and perilous task. Philosophical and personal biases affect methods decisions. Limitations of time and money constrain the evaluator in the selection of research methods. The evaluator's capabilities are also a powerful influence in the decision process. The starting point in this decision process, however, is recognition that there are methods options. If evaluators are to consider seriously a variety of methods options, they must possess a substantial repertoire of research skills.

This book has been aimed at increasing and expanding the methods repertoire of evaluators. No attempt has been made here to argue that qualitative methods are "better" than quantitative methods. The purpose of this book has been to help those evaluators who want to employ qualitative methods to know when it is appropriate to do so, and to know how to use qualitative methods in ways that will produce useful and valid data.

For Further Reading

Filstead, W. J. (Ed.). (1970). *Qualitative methodology.* Chicago: Markham.

Guba, E. G., & Lincoln, Y. S. (1981). *Effective evaluation: Improving the usefulness of evaluation results through responsive and naturalistic approaches.* San Francisco: Jossey-Bass.

House, E. (1980). *Evaluating with validity.* Newbury Park, CA: Sage.

Kirk, J., & Miller, M. (1986). *Reliability and validity in qualitative research.* Newbury Park, CA: Sage.

Kuhn, T. (1970). *The structure of scientific revolutions.* Chicago: University of Chicago Press.

Lincoln, Y. S., & Guba, E. G. (1985). *Naturalistic inquiry.* Newbury Park, CA: Sage.

Reichardt, C. S., & Cook, T. D. (1979). Beyond qualitative versus quantitative methods. In T. Cook & C. S. Reichardt (Eds.), *Qualitative and quantitative methods.* Newbury Park, CA: Sage.

Scriven, M. (1972). Objectivity and subjectivity in educational research. In L. G. Thomas (Ed.), *Philosophical redirection of educational research: The seventy-first yearbook of the National Society for the Study of Education.* Chicago: University of Chicago Press.

Trend, M. G. (1978). On the reconciliation of qualitative and quantitative analyses: A case study. *Human Organization, 37,* 345-354.

References

Alkin, M. C. (1972). Wider context goals and goal-based evaluators. *Evaluation Comment: The Journal of Educational Evaluation, 3-4*(December), 10-11.

Alkin, M. C. (with Burry, J.). (1985). *A guide for evaluation decision makers.* Newbury Park, CA: Sage.

Barker, R. G. (1968). *Ecological psychology.* Stanford: Stanford University Press.

Becker, H., & Geer, B. (1970). Participant observation and interviewing: A comparison. In W. J. Filstead (Ed.), *Qualitative methodology.* Chicago: Markham.

Bogdan, R., & Taylor, S. J. (1975). *Introduction to qualitative methods.* New York: John Wiley.

Boruch, R., & Rindskopf, D. (1984). Data analysis. In L. Rutman (Ed.), Evaluation research methods (2nd ed., pp. 121-158). Newbury Park, CA: Sage. Bruyn, S. (1966). *The human perspective in sociology: The methodology of participant observation.* Englewood Cliffs, NJ: Prentice-Hall.

Bussis, A., Chittenden, E. A., & Amarel, M. (1973). *Methodology in educational evaluation and research.* Princeton, NJ: Educational Testing Service. (mimeo)

Carini, P. F. (1975). *Observation and description: An alternative methodology for the investigation of human phenomena.* Grand Forks: University of North Dakota Press.

Cervantes Saavedra, M. D. (1964). *Don Quixote.* New York: Signet Classics.

Cronbach, L. J. (1975). Beyond the two disciplines of scientific psychology. *American Psychologist, 30,* 116-127.

Cronbach, L. J. (1980). *Toward reform of program evaluation.* San Francisco: Jossey-Bass.

Cronbach, L. J. (1982). *Designing evaluations of educational and social programs.* San Francisco: Jossey-Bass.

Denzin, N. K. (1978a). The logic of naturalistic inquiry. In N. K. Denzin (Ed.), *Sociological methods: A sourcebook.* New York: McGraw-Hill.

Denzin, N. K. (1978b). *The research act.* New York: McGraw-Hill.

Deutscher, I. (1970). Words and deeds: Social science and social policy. In W. J. Filstead (Ed.), *Qualitative methodology.* Chicago: Markham.

Dewey, J. (1956). *The child and the curriculum.* Chicago: University of Chicago Press.

Douglas, J. D. (1976). *Investigative social research: Individual and team field research.* Newbury Park, CA: Sage.

Fetterman, D. M. (Ed.). (1984). *Ethnography in educational evaluation.* Newbury Park, CA: Sage.

Fielding, N., & Fielding, J. (1986). *Linking data.* Newbury Park, CA: Sage.

Filstead, W. J. (Ed.). (1970). *Qualitative methodology.* Chicago: Markham.

Frake, C. (1962). The Ethnographic study of cognitive systems. In T. Gladwin & W. H. Sturtevant (Eds.), *Anthropology and human behavior.* Washington, DC: Anthropology Society.

Garfinkel, H. (1967). *Studies in ethnomethodology.* Englewood Cliffs, NJ: Prentice-Hall.

Glaser, B. G., & Strauss, A. L. (1967). *Discovery of grounded theory: Strategies for qualitative research.* Chicago: AVC.

Guba, E. G. (1978). *Toward a methodology of naturalistic inquiry in educational evaluation* (CSE Monograph Series in Evaluation No. 8). Los Angeles: Center for the Study of Evaluation.

Guba, E. G., & Lincoln, Y. S. (1981). *Effective evaluation: Improving the usefulness of evaluation results through responsive and naturalistic approaches.* San Francisco: Jossey-Bass.

Hage, J. (1972). *Techniques and problems of theory construction in sociology.* New York: John Wiley.

Hedges, A. (1985). Group interviewing. In R. Walker (Ed.), *Applied qualitative research.* Brookfield, VT: Gower.

House, E. (1980). *Evaluating with validity.* Newbury Park, CA: Sage.

Human Service Research Institute. (1984). *Assessing and enhancing the quality of human services.* Boston, MA: Author.

Johnson, J. M. (1975). *Doing field research.* New York: Free Press.

Joint Committee on Standards for Educational Evaluation. (1981). *Standards for evaluations of educational programs, projects, and materials.* New York: McGraw-Hill.

Jones, S. (1985). Depth interviewing. In R. Walker (Ed.), *Applied qualitative research.* Brookfield, VT: Gower.

Junker, B. H. (1960). *Field work: An introduction to the social sciences.* Chicago: University of Chicago Press.

Katzer, J., Cook, K. H., & Crouch, W. W. (1978). *Evaluating information: A guide for users of social science research.* Reading, MA: Addison-Wesley.

Kirk, J., & Miller, M. (1986). *Reliability and validity in qualitative research.* Newbury Park, CA: Sage.

Kuhn, T. (1970). *The structure of scientific revolutions.* Chicago: University of Chicago Press.

Lalonde, B. (1982). Quality assurance. *Handbook on mental health administration.* San Francisco: Jossey-Bass.

Lang, K., & Lang, G. E. (1960). Decisions for Christ: Billy Graham in New York. In M. Stein, A. J. Vidich, & D. M. White (Eds.), *Identity and anxiety.* New York: Free Press.

Lincoln, Y. S., & Guba, E. G. (1985). *Naturalistic inquiry.* Newbury Park, CA: Sage.

Lofland, J. (1971). *Analyzing social settings.* Belmont, CA: Wadsworth.

Merton, R., Fiske, M., & Kendall, P. L. (1956). *The focused interview.* New York: Free Press.

Miles, M., & Huberman, M. (1984). *Qualitative data analysis.* Newbury Park, CA: Sage.

Patton, M. Q. (1980a). Making methods choices. *Evaluation and program planning, 3,* 219-228.

Patton, M. Q. (1980b). *Qualitative evaluation methods.* Newbury Park, CA: Sage.

Patton, M. Q. (1986). *Utilization-focused evaluation.* Newbury Park, CA: Sage.

Payne, S. L. (1951). *The art of asking questions.* Princeton, NJ: Princeton University Press.

Pelto, P. J., & Pelto, G. H. (1978). *Anthropological research: The structure of inquiry.* Cambridge: Cambridge University Press.

Powdermaker, H. (1966). *Stranger and friend.* New York: Norton.

Reichardt, C. S., & Cook, T. D. (1979). Beyond qualitative versus quantitative methods. In T. Cook & C. S. Reichardt (Eds.), *Qualitative and quantitative methods.* Newbury Park, CA: Sage.

Richardson, S. A., Dohrenwend, B. S., & Klein, D. (1965). *Interviewing: Its forms and functions*. New York: Basic Books.

Rutman, L. (1980). *Planning useful evaluations: Evaluability assessments*. Newbury Park, CA: Sage.

Scriven, M. (1972a). Pros and cons about goal-free evaluation. *Evaluation Comment, 3,* 1-7.

Scriven, M. (1972b). Objectivity and subjectivity in educational research. In L. G. Thomas (Ed.), *Philosophical redirection of educational research: The seventy-first yearbook of the National Society for the Study of Education*. Chicago: University of Chicago Press.

Shapiro, E. (1973). Educational evaluation: Rethinking the criteria of competence. *School Review,* (November), 523-549.

Shils, E. A. (1959). A social inquiry and the autonomy of the individual. In D. Lerner (Ed.), The human meaning of the social sciences. Cleveland, OH: Meridian.

Stake, R. E. (1975). *Evaluating the arts in education: A responsive approach*. Columbus, OH: Charles E. Merrill.

Stenhous, L. (1977). *Case study as a basis for research in a theoretical contemporary history of education*. East Anglia, England: Centre for Applied Research in Education.

Strike, K. (1972). Explaining and understanding: The impact of science on our concept of man. In L. G. Thomas (Ed.), *Philosophical redirection of educational research: The seventy-first yearbook of the National Society for the Study of Education*. Chicago: University of Chicago Press.

Trend, M. G. (1978). On the reconciliation of qualitative and quantitative analyses: A case study. *Human Organization, 37,* 345-354.

Walker, R. (Ed.). (1985) *Applied qualitative research*. Brookfield, VT: Gower.

Wax, R. H. (1971). *Doing fieldwork: Warnings and advice.* Chicago: University of Chicago Press.

Webb. E. J., Campbell, D. T., Schwartz, R., & Sechrest, L. (1966). *Unobtrusive measures: Nonreactive research in the social sciences*. Chicago: Rand McNally.

Weiss, C. (1972). *Evaluation research*. Englewood Cliffs, NJ: Prentice-Hall.

Werner, O., & Schoepfle, M. (1987). *Systematic fieldwork* (Vols. 1-2). Newbury Park, CA: Sage.

Wholey, J. (1979). *Evaluation: Promise and performance*. Washington, DC: The Urban Institute.

Willems, E. P., & Raush, H. L. (1969). *Naturalistic viewpoints in psychological research*. New York: Holt, Rinehart & Winston.

Williams, W. (1976). Implementation analysis and assessment. In W. Williams & R. F. Elmore (Eds.), *Social program implementation*. New York: Academic Press.

Wolf, R. L., & Tymitz, B. (1977). Whatever happened to the giant wombat: An investigation of the impact of the Ice Age Mammals and Emergence of Man Exhibit. Washington, DC: National Museum of Natural History, Smithsonian Institute. (mimeo)

Index